MANNERS
FOR WOMEN

D1479387

BY MRS. HUMPHRY
("MADGE" OF "TRUTH")

Author of
"MANNERS FOR MEN"

Webb&Bower
EXETER, ENGLAND

Published in Great Britain 1979 by
Webb & Bower (Publishers) Limited,
33 Southernhay East, Exeter, Devon, EX1 1NS

Distributed by WHS Distributors
(a division of W. H. Smith and Son Limited)
Euston Street, Freeman's Common, Aylestone Road,
Leicester LE2 7SS

Designed by Vic Giolitto

MANNERS FOR WOMEN first published 1897

This edition with additional material © Webb & Bower
(Publishers) Limited/Michael Levien 1979

ISBN 0 906671 01 9

Printed and bound in Great Britain by
Butler and Tanner Limited, Frome, Somerset

FOREWORD TO THE FACSIMILE EDITION

In her day Mrs Humphry, a popular London author and journalist, was unsurpassed on the subject of etiquette. Her *Manners for Women* quickly became a best-seller, for it had everything the modern woman needed to know concerning correct social behaviour in town and country. Of course times have changed; since the book first appeared war and revolution have stood society on its head; even the word "lady" has come to be used indiscriminately. Women today are surely little troubled by their imperfection at curtsying or with the way they laugh. "The laugh," says Mrs Humphry, "is a test of good breeding and cultivation." And in an age of trouser-suits and topless bathing who cares about bicycling dresses, or the "half-low" bodices that were all the rage at smart seaside theatres? Yet there is more to it than that, and the social content of this book, threaded with wisps of irony and humour, brings back into focus a whole epoch – a period of many subtleties and courtesies and restraints which, harmonizing with one another, produced a pattern of conduct whose graciousness would be hard to match. The author offers fascinating tips on many topics, from food and present-giving to the gentle art of snubbing. In the quarter-century since I acquired a copy of *Manners for Women*, now reproduced in facsimile, society has undergone a further transformation. Yet the answer to the beguiling question "Can anything in the world be nicer than a really nice girl?" is, abidingly, the same.

MICHAEL LEVIEN   *Totnes, Devon 1979*

CONTENTS

MANNERS FOR WOMEN.

THE GIRL IN SOCIETY.

CAN anything in the world be nicer than a really nice girl ? She is full of contradictions and often "set with little wilful thorns," but where would her charm be if she were plainly to be read by all comers ?

Some one has said that woman is one of Nature's agreeable blunders, and every one is so tired of hearing about this particular blunder, in fullest detail, from her tight-waisted corset to her love of chocolate creams; from her fear of a mouse or spider to her terrible strong-mindedness; from her silly frivolity to her disagreeable earnestness; that it is worth while for once to **The typical English girl.** endeavour to depict the typical English girl as we see her every day. She is to no one more conspicuously a blunder than to herself, and to no one more than herself is she an incomprehensible puzzle. But she is usually healthy-minded, and therefore not given unduly to intro-

spection. She is far too well occupied
in enjoying herself—riding her bicycle,
punting herself about on the river,
playing tennis or golf, and making sun-
shine in her home—to have much time
for profitless self-analysis. She reads
often enough that the sex she belongs
to is a mystery, a problem, and she is
content to leave herself unsolved, like
a difficult conundrum. She is bright,
frank, good-natured, merry, modest,
and simple. What a pity to spoil her,
as so many mothers do. It is pure
waste, and a cruelty to boot, for spoiled
girls, even more than spoiled boys,
have to learn their lessons in a bitter
school from a shrewish teacher. And
they might have been taught them
with love and gentleness in the home.

But the ideal girl is not
spoiled, though she has her
faults. She is undoubtedly
hard-hearted. How can she
be sympathetic with trouble and sorrow
when she has never known either ?
She will soften by and by, and will
wonder at her own hardness when she
was seventeen or eighteen. She can
sorrow keenly over a fallen horse, a
hurt dog, or a dying kitten ; but she
fails to realise the subtler phases of
grief or pain. She will comprehend
but too keenly later on in life, but in
girlhood she must be admitted to be
hard.

The happy girls of the century-end
have not such good reason for wishing

*She is un-
doubtedly
hard-hearted.*

to be boys as their mothers, and, more still, their grandmothers, had in their young days. The tyrannous needle swallowed up their youth. When they were not sewing "white work" in long seams, with such mysterious rites as counter-hemming, running and felling, top-sewing and pointing, they were busy at embroidery frames, producing impossible pictures in tent and tapestry stitch. At seven years of age our poor dear little great-grandmothers were set down to their samplers. They were cruelly used by those samplers. Some of these that have survived make the humane shudder. Mothers of the present moment are probably just a little too tender-hearted, and forget what admirable training, what remarkable development of fine qualities, are involved in the accomplishment of a difficult piece of work. But those elaborate borders were too cruel. Think of the endless unpicking of false stitches, of the counting three up and three down in those small vandykes, of the tearful eyes that did the counting, and the little, plump, tired fingers that handled the weary samplers day after day for months and months. Those poor little great-grandmothers!

The modern girl escapes the tyranny of the needle.

The girl of to-day hardly knows what Berlin wool-work means. She has probably heard of the crewels that entered into the plan of her mother's girlhood, but fancy-work plays no part whatever in her own cheery, breezy, young existence. Very often she ignores even the needle of ordinary life, and her thimble knows her so little that it will not come when it is called. It has been left in waste places. But the best and nicest of our English girls can use the needle quite as cleverly as they can wield a pair of sculls or handle the reins or manage a bicycle. The sewing-machine, at which her mother spent hours of every week in her own young years, has no hold whatever upon our English girl. She has escaped it. If she wishes she were a boy, it is not for pure weariness of indoor life, such as her ancestresses must have felt for many and many a generation back. Girls now have a full, free life opening out before them, and the widening of the prospect is occasionally dazzling. They are going to do such great things. The glow and glory of them quite blinds the eyes to the small things that lie close at hand. They make up their minds to be a Florence Nightingale, and, while revelling in the prospect, forget that it is time for mother to have her medicine or father his beef-tea. It is things like these that make girls so puzzling to themselves and others.

But she can use it as well as the sculls.

The girl of to-day, with her fine physical development, her bright, cheery nature, and her robust contempt for all things small and mean, is an

4

immense improvement on the girl of

The girl of to-day an immense improvement on the girl of yesterday. yesterday or the day before. She is as the plant grown out of doors in congenial soil, with plenty of sunshine and careful tending, compared with one that has been nurtured in a hot-house. Instead of the maudlin sensibility that was fashionable in the days of Berlin work, she has a vigorous contempt for all forms of softness. Just as her hands are inured to such hardness as enables them to contribute to her amusement in rowing, "biking," and the like, her mind and character are strung up to a firmness of which a sentimental heroine of fifty years since would have been thoroughly ashamed. Cry at a wedding? Not she. She would consider it idiotic, and, indeed, I am not sure that she would not call it "blubbing," as her brother does. She entertains a fine, manly feeling of friendship for her father, and is a good comrade with her brothers, sharing in most of their sports and pastimes.

She is thoroughly healthy. Her nerves are in a very different condition from that in which the indoor girl of a generation since found hers. In a word, she is thoroughly healthy, and shows it not only in the elasticity of her steps and the erectness of her carriage, but in her clear complexion, bright eyes, glossy hair, and glowing lips.

What about accomplishments? Well, thank goodness, the piano is going out of fashion for girls in the best circles. They are taught just enough of it to let them find out whether or no they have a taste for it. If they have, they go on with it ; if not, it is given up, to the great easement of humanity.

About "accomplishments."

In the same way, drawing and painting are no longer considered indispensable to the equipment of a girl for living her life. Her chief accomplishments are waltzing and tennis-playing.

To speak French is not exactly regarded as an accomplishment nowadays any more than gloves are considered a luxury. Fluent French has become a necessity in social life of any status. A little German and Italian are almost necessary as well in these days of constant continental travel, and the usual plan for enabling the tall daughter of the century-end to acquire these is the pleasant one of taking her abroad for a few weeks of every spring.

The Prince and Princess of Wales and their children usually converse in French, and they have visiting cards printed in that language in addition to those in English. Those in French are used in the interchange of visits to all foreign Powers, as well as at the various Embassies, French being the recognised language of polite society all over Europe.

DECADENCE OF THE CURTSEY.

GIRLS are never taught to curtsey now, as they used to be. A real, old-fashioned "courtesy," as it used to be spelled, is quite an elaborate performance. First, you draw back the right foot, getting it straight

The old-fashioned curtsey. behind the other, and down you go, as far as the suppleness of your limbs will

permit, coming up to the "recover" with all the weight on the right foot, and the left pointed out most daintily. A curtsey is about the only thing in the world that is helped out by the high-heeled shoe. The only trace of this old-fashioned and very graceful bit of deportment is the deep reverence made by the ladies at Her Majesty's Drawing-Rooms. Some of them perform it with practiced *aplomb*. Others never achieve it. There is a very pretty young princess who plumps down with an alarming suddenness that always makes the Royal circle covertly smile. Even when making the ordinary "bob" to Royalty on less ceremonious occasions, this lovely girl strikes her heel against the floor with a bump that seems to have arrived straight

7

from the maddest moment of a merry breakdown. A well-known duchess curtseys with such infinite grace, repeating it before the various members of the Royal circle at Drawing-Rooms, that the Queen's eyes invariably follow her with a glance of pleased approbation. A handsome countess of regal appearance makes a very imposing obeisance, but it is too stiff to be really graceful. Among the numerous Americans presented, some carry themselves into the presence of Royalty with a truly republican air of equality and fraternity, contenting themselves with bowing to the Queen, as they would to their hostess of an afternoon reception. Others who have studied the matter more deeply sink low with a willowy grace, just brushing with their lips the plump little white hand extended to them, then rising with a slightly backward movement that seems to accept dismissal and tacitly to disclaim any desire to unnecessary intrusion. "Quite theatrical!" said a very plump dowager of such a performance. Every one else had admired it. But perhaps the consciousness of an over-allowance of adipose tissue and blooming plumptitude, had rendered the dear lady inappreciative of slender grace and languorous ease in others.

The Queen is a lover of beauty, and a keen judge of it, both in form and face. The *débutante* whose appearance evokes a word of pleased comment from Her Majesty is always safe to be one of the beauties of her first season. And the Royal memory for faces is an excellent one. Any one who has had an opportunity of seeing the Queen walk through the lane of guests at a Royal garden party, Royal concert, or at any public function, will remember the glances cast from side to side, noting every face, keenly alive and discerning, awake to every circumstance and incident. When listening to addresses or long speeches an expression of weariness, sometimes amounting to indifference and even apathy, occasionally settles down on the Royal countenance. Oh, those long addresses! How many years of Her Majesty's life would be totalled up if the bad quarters of an hour spent in hearing addresses were laid end to end and make up into one huge sum of patient endurance? But when face to face with her people the Queen is full of quick perception.

Characteristics of the Queen.

So beauty and grace do not go unrecognised at our Court of England. Nor do less agreeable characteristics. The lady who favoured our Queen and her family with affable little nods and warmly shook hands with the Sovereign at one famous Drawing-Room is not yet forgotten, and has been the cause of many a hearty laugh. Another, the

Incidents at Court.

9

heel of whose shoe caught in her skirts, and who could not get up after her curtsey, and had to be carried from the Presence Chamber after the fashion of the old game of "Honey pots," caused etiquette to be forgotten at the strictest Court in the world, a broad smile appearing on the Queen's own face, while the young princesses tittered irrepressibly, and the Princess of Wales bit her pretty lips. The Prince looked as if he longed to give one of his great guffaws. Another memorable lady lost part of her bodice, and had to retire hastily in much confusion, wrapping herself in her train. All these incidents are remembered and credited to the correct names by one whose mind is not so much "ta'en up wi' the things o' the State," as not to reserve a shelf for minor matters.

The Royal disapprobation of cosmetics, hair-dyes, and other forms of insincerity in personal appearance is not veiled in any way. To the application, or mis-application, of rouge society has become hardened, but when it is plastered on in quantities that defeat the very object of deception, for which it is used, a little open comment from those in high places has worked wonders in reducing the evil. The cosmetic epidemic comes and goes like Bob Acres' courage, but, unlike it, will never wholly disappear.

Insincerity in personal appearance.

LEARNING TO LAUGH.

MISS FLORENCE ST. JOHN told the world once in the pages of a Sunday paper how she learnt to laugh.

Florence St. John's laugh. Mr. Farnie, she says, took her in hand for the laughing scene in " Madame Favart," and made her sing a descending octave staccato with the syllables Ha, ha ! The actress rehearsed it over and over again, and on the night of the production found herself perfectly *au fait.* Any one who has ever heard Miss Florence St. John's pretty laugh on the stage, will admit that it was worth taking some pains to achieve. A curious thing about laughing is that when it has really a hearty sound it often re-acts upon one, and though it is but an empty echo, it suggests the sense of mirth which ought properly to have inspired it. There are many reasons why the careful

The culture of the laugh. culture of the laugh should be attended to. The theatre is the very best place to study the matter when an amusing piece is being played. Look round at your neighbours in the stalls or dress circle, good friends, and see how many of them know how to indulge themselves in the expression of their mirth. For every one whose laughter is melodious, there will be found a dozen who merely grin and half-a-dozen whose sole relief is in physical contortion. Some of the latter bend forward, folding themselves almost double, then spring back again, and repeat this jerky and ridiculous movement afresh at every joke. Others throw their heads back in a way that disagreeably suggests dislocation. A few are so put to it to give vent to their overwhelming sense of amusement that they violently slap themselves, twisting about the while as though they were undergoing tortures. Cachinnations in every key resound on all sides, varying from the shrill and attenuated " He ! he !" to the double chuckle " Ho ! ho !" fired off, like postmen's knocks, at tremendous speed, so as to be ready, decks cleared, for the next joke. Cackling suggestive of the farmyard, and snorts not un-reminiscent of pig-styes, produce variety.

As to the grins, very few of them can be, in the remotest sense of the word, described as pleasing.

On "grins." Pretty teeth may redeem some of them from absolute ignominy, but, as a rule, the exhibition of whole meadows of pale pink gum is inconsonant with one's ideas of beauty. The silent grin is perhaps the most absurd and unpardonable mode of expressing mirth, and it enforces more than ever the lesson that laughing should, if its expression does not come by nature, be carefully taught. Nor need there be any artificiality in this, for, after a while, it becomes as natural as the correct pronunciation of words after a series of elocution lessons, and, as everybody knows, distinct enunciation does not come by nature. But who could describe it as artificial? In the same way the pretty harmonious laugh is a second nature with many.

A word of warning. The only thing to be guarded against is that the inculcated laugh is apt to grow stereotyped, and few things are more irritating than to hear it over and over again, begin on the same note, run down the same scale, and consequently express no more mirth than the keys of the piano.

There is no greater ornament to conversation than the ripple of silvery notes that forms the perfect laugh. It makes the person who evokes it feel pleased with himself, and even invests what he has said with a charm of wit and humour which might not be otherwise observed. There is in London artistic society a lady whose beautiful voice is generally admired. She laughs on two soft contralto notes, and, limited as they are, there is no more genuine or musical expression of mirth to be heard anywhere than hers.

Sarah Bernhardt, with her *voix d'or*, has an incomparable *rire d'argent*. Rythmically melodious as it is, it is not so infectiously genuine as her pathos and her real tears. The latter are unmistakable. I have often seen them on the face of the great tragédienne when she has played Frou-frou or Marguerite in the "Dame aux Camélias." No doubt she was taught to laugh as part of her dramatic education. Why should not mothers avail themselves of the idea for the benefit of the nursery and the schoolroom? Children of tender years are naturally shrill, and it is only by constant checking that this tendency is averted. Even in speech they fall into all sorts of extraordinary ways of expressing mirth. For one child who laughs naturally and musically there are half a dozen who grunt, chuckle, or almost scream. As to schoolgirls their giggling is proverbial. They would be always laughing if they might, and, as this would considerably interfere with school discipline, governesses have to make a rule against it, with the consequence that when the merry young things do laugh it is with a furtive secrecy. This produces the giggle and the titter, and actually destroys all spontaneity in the expression of mirth. Then comes the mother's opportunity, not only in eliminating

A hint for the nursery.

Giggling and Tittering.

14

bad habits in the audible laugh, but also in the contortions of the facial muscles, which sometimes are quite painful to witness, to say nothing of being extremely hideous.

Charles Lamb said of some one that he was "awkward in his face." There are many who share **Laughter a test of good breeding.** this defect; but for every one of them there are hundreds who are awkward in their laughter. And it might so easily be mended. The laugh is a test of good breeding and cultivation. It expresses refinement, or its absence, as clearly as the voice and intonation. The coarse " Haw-haw " of the uneducated tells us much. But it is music itself as compared with the horrid luscious laugh of the man who appreciates a nasty innuendo, the hateful *double-entendre* of the music hall. That is one of the most odious sounds in a world of dreary noises.

So much for the visibilities and audibilities of laughter. What of the thing itself? Does not man share its capacity with the gods? Does any meaner animal laugh? Some quibbler may suggest the hyæna or the laughing jackass, but such frivolous objections must not be taken in earnest. Man is the only animal that can express mirth in appropriate sound. It is, therefore, a prerogative. But do we make as much of it as we might? There are whole days when one never laughs. In ordinary circumstances this amounts to neglecting a privilege. Doctors tell us that laughter defeats the spleen, stimulates the circulation, improves the digestion, and reacts most favourably upon the health. And is it not much pleasanter than any other kind of medicine ? Why do we not take our agreeable doses oftener ? The muscles relax, the atmosphere of the mind brightens. The laugh comes, and the whole being is braced and strengthened.

The physical importance of laughter.

The sense of humour is cultivable. But how often does one set oneself to cultivate it, either individually or in others ? Every mature man or woman is aware of the influences that have come into his life in this respect. Association with those who are quickly awake to the humorous aspect of things is the best means of becoming so ourselves. It is delightful to arouse and develop this sense in children. They are very quick to learn in the school of wit and humour ; and often overpass the teacher in their readiness to see the ridiculous and appreciate its fun. It is not difficult to keep it within the banks of geniality, and prevent it from overflowing into the sandy desert of satirical and cynical mirth, so-called. From this latter variety

The sense of humour can be cultivated.

comes the detestable practical joke, never to be sufficiently deprecated or contemned. In reality it is often a species of " man's inhumanity to man."

"A laugh is worth a hundred groans in any market," said Henry Ward Beecher ; and he was not the first discoverer of the value of cheerfulness.

> "The merry heart goes all the day,
> The sad tires in a mile-a."

So wrote Shakespeare, who best knew the Castle of Man's Heart.

IN THE STREET.

ONE can almost invariably distinguish the well-bred girl at the first glance, whether she is walking, shopping, in an omnibus, descending from a carriage or a cab, or sauntering up and down in the Park. Though the fashionable manner inclines to a rather marked decisiveness and the fashionable voice to loudness, even harshness, there is a quiet self-possession about the gentlewoman, whether young or old, that marks her out from women of a lower class, whose manner is florid. This is perhaps the best word to describe the lively gestures, the notice-attracting glance and the self-conscious air of the underbred, who continually appear to wish to impress their personality upon all they meet.

A gentlewoman is known by her quiet self-possession.

Self-effacement is as much the rule of good manners in the street as it is in society. The well-bred woman goes quietly along, intent on her own business and regardless of the rest of the world, except in so far as to keep from intruding upon their personal rights.

Self-effacement in the street as imperative as in Society.

18

IN THE STREET.

This is another test of the well-bred woman. A delicate sense of self-respect keeps her from contact with her neighbour in train or tramcar or omnibus, so for as such contact may be avoidable. The woman of the lower classes may spread her arms, lean up against her neighbour, or in other ways behave with a disagreeable familiarity ; the gentlewoman never.

There was a good old rule of manners that forbade a lady to look back after any one in the street, or to turn and stare at any one in church, opera, theatre, or concert room. These good old rules seem fast to be becoming obsolete ; or so one might suppose from the frequency with which they are disregarded.

BICYCLING.

THE etiquette of bicycling has often been discussed. It seems simple enough, especially to those who are

The etiquette of bicycling. familiar with the rule of the road in riding or driving. But thousands of bicyclists belong to a class which is ignorant of the charms of horse exercise, and they may be unaware that the rule of the

The rule of the road for bicycling. road is exactly the opposite to that which guides pedestrians on the footpath. All riders keep to the left. In passing other bicyclists or vehicles that are in advance, a *détour* is made to the right ; but in meeting traffic of any kind the rider keeps close to the left. When wheeling with a man, the girl bicyclist will probably be given the safer side of the road. He would keep on her right in ordinary traffic, so as to be between her and approaching vehicles.

A little thoughtfulness for others would suggest to all wheelwomen that

Passing invalids and children. to ride very rapidly past invalids in bath chairs or parties of children who are in front of her, sounding the bell sharply and suddenly in their ears, is a bit of bad manners. It is also

Passing other vehicles. well to exercise prudence in passing other vehicles, remembering that one risks not only one's own safety but imperils that of others by attempting anything rash. Not very long ago a woman on a bicycle, in endeavouring to cut in between an approaching four-in-hand and a cart, caused a terrible accident in which the coach was overturned, several people (including herself) were badly hurt, and a couple of valuable horses so badly damaged that they had to be shot. A little prudence would have prevented this and would certainly have counted as good manners.

The bicycle is responsible for much promiscuous acquaintanceship, but as

Promiscuous acquaintance. that is a subject which I have very fully treated in " Manners for Men," I will say nothing of it here.

CARDS AND CALLS.

It used to be the rule that so long as a girl was unmarried and lived at home, even when, though she **The old rule on visiting cards.** might have reached the indefinite age of "spinsterhood," she had no separate visiting card, but shared that of her mother, under whose name her own appeared. But now there have been such wide openings for girls and women, and in a large family there are often such different pursuits and occupations taken up by the various members, that the old rule has become partly obsolete. It still holds good in high society, however, until the girl ceases to be exactly a girl, and enters upon a period of life that may perhaps be described as "obviously mature." **Exemption from the rule.** She may have struck out a line of her own and have a perfectly different circle of acquaintances from that of her mother. She may be actively a philanthropist, or may identify herself with politics or the pursuit of science. Or she may become a great traveller, wandering far over the world, away from her mother and her mother's visiting cards.

CARDS AND CALLS.

"The old order changeth" indeed, but still, for the most part, the old rule holds good that keeps a girl under the maternal wing for the first years of her social life.

Should she have no mother, her card would bear her own name, or, if she have sisters, it would read **"Should she have no mother."** "The Misses" before the surname. Should an aunt or other female relative be living with and chaperoning her, the aunt's name would appear above that of the girl's.

The etiquette of card-leaving frequently alters in minor details, but in the following particulars have been unchanged for very many years. The card must be a thin white piece of pasteboard, absolutely plain, without border or ornament of any kind. The name occupies the centre, **Form of the card.** and is always in copperplate italic characters. The address is in rather smaller characters of the same description, and its correct position is in the lower left-hand corner. The size of the card is exactly $3\frac{1}{2}$ by $2\frac{1}{2}$ inches. Sometimes the particulars of the "At Home" day are printed on it ; sometimes merely written. The "day" set apart for receiving calls is essentially a middle-class custom, and a very **The "At Home" day.** sensible and useful one. Great ladies with carriages and plenty of leisure have no difficulty in calling on their friends, but in the upper middle-classes there is not always great wealth or much leisure, and the institution of the "At Home" day is a most valuable one. In London it is especially so, in view of the long distances one has to cover in making calls.

The etiquette of the visiting card, though simple enough, is sometimes misunderstood. In making a call, the visitor does not send in her card if her acquaintance should be at home, but only leaves it on departure, or if the friend is out. A married woman leaves two of her husband's cards, with one of her own. Of the two, one is meant for the lady called upon, the other for her husband. Should she be unmarried or a widow, the caller leaves only one of her husband's cards.

The etiquette of card-leaving.

THE ENGAGED GIRL.

IT is usual, when a girl becomes engaged, for a short time to elapse before
the affair is announced, ex-
cept to the most intimate
friends of both parties.
This is a precaution against
the inconveniences and disagreeables
of broken engagements. But when the
affair has become fairly well "cemen-
ted," as it were, and the time fixed
for the marriage approaches, it is usual
for the mother of the engaged girl to
have a dinner party, at which the
fiancé is introduced to the friends of
the family. This dinner is often followed by an evening party, with
a similar object in view. Or an
afternoon "At Home" is occasionally held sufficient to answer all
purposes.

The bride-elect usually visits her
future husband's family shortly after

*The engage-
ment not
announced
immediately.*

her engagement. This is often a
rather trying time, for she knows she
is the object of very critical
Visiting the future husband's family. examination on the part of
her prospective mother-in-
law and sisters-in-law, to
say nothing of father-in-law and
brothers-in-law. Many an intended
marriage has been broken off after
the *fiancée's* visit to her intended husband's family. Mothers have an idea
that no girl is good enough for their
sons, and though sisters do not always
share that opinion, they are inclined
to resent the absorption of
Often a pain-ful ordeal. the brother in another girl.
Consequently all is not roses
during such a visit. A gentle, lovable
girl, however, frequently wins golden
opinions on such occasions, especially if she be of the unselfish sort,
and does not wholly monopolise the
time and attention of the son of the
house.

When the engagement has become
an accepted fact the *fiancée* writes to
her friends and tells them about it.
Should she be motherless,
Announcing the engagement. she must write to the elders,
announcing her engagement,
but otherwise this task is
always undertaken by the mother.
With distant acquaintances
Respecting distant acquaintances. it is unnecessary to write
until the day is fixed and
invitations are being sent
out, and not even then if they are

not to receive invitations to the wedding. In fact, it is in better taste not to do so, as it would look like suggesting a wedding present. It is this very thing that makes such notes extremely difficult to write. And it also imports an element of embarrassment into the selection of invited guests for the wedding.

Invitations are sent out on white cards with silver lettering. The shapes of these are various, *Invitation cards.* and sometimes, like ordinary invitations, those to weddings are on sheets of oblong note-sized paper, which fold over and fasten down with a gummed flap. Any one wishing to be perfectly up-to-date in all such matters should send or go to some first-class firm, such as Parkins and Gotto, where they will ascertain what are the customs of the best society in all that regards invitations, notepaper, and the whole environment of correspondence. There they will learn that the *Simplicity of fashionable usage.* "upper ten" hardly ever use their crests on note-paper, invitations, or Christmas greeting cards ; that many-coloured monograms and large lettering in addresses are equally out of favour, and that the supremacy of good, thick, white, plain, cream-laid notepaper and envelopes is maintained.

Form of the invitation card. Invitations to weddings usually take the following form :—

MR. and MRS. JONES

Request the pleasure of

MR. and MRS. ROBINSON'S

Company at the

Marriage

of their Daughter GERALDINE and

MR. ALFRED SMITH,

at

Saint Paul's, Knightsbridge,

On Thursday, June 30th, at 2.30 P.M.,

and afterwards

at

200, Cadogan Place.

Usually, the whole of this is ready printed, with the exception of the names of the guests.

All answers to invitations should be framed as nearly as possible **Answers to invitations.** upon the lines of the invitations themselves. Thus, the correct reply to the above would be :

Mr. and Mrs. Robinson have much pleasure in accepting Mr. and Mrs. Jones' kind invitation to the marriage of their daughter on Thursday, June 30th, and afterwards at 200. Cadogan Place.

Should the invited guests intend to be present at the church, but **For partial acceptance.** not at the reception, she must convey as much in reply. For instance :

Miss Smith has much pleasure in accepting Mrs. Brown's kind invitation to be present at her daughter's marriage on Thursday, at St. Paul's, but regrets that a previous engagement will prevent her attending the reception at Cadogan Place.

Or :

Miss Smith accepts with pleasure Mrs. Brown's kind invitation for Thursday afternoon at 200, Cadogan Place, on the occasion of her daughter's marriage, but regrets that a previous engagement will prevent her from being present at the ceremony.

In declining an invitation it is not so necessary to specify day **Declining an invitation.** and hour as it is in accepting, the idea in doing so being to assure the host or hostess that the guest is quite clear on the matter of date and time.

THE wedding breakfast is now almost a thing of the past, having been superseded by the recep-

Receptions superseding breakfasts. tion or wedding tea since the extension of the canonical hours for the celebration of marriage. I append a few menus, including that given at White Lodge on the occasion of the marriage of the Duchess of York. All wedding menus are printed in silver, whether relating to breakfasts or afternoon receptions.

The following was the menu at the Duchess of York's wed-

A fashionable menu. ding reception at White Lodge :

MENU.

SANDWICHES.

Foies Gras.   Saumon Fumé.
Pain Bis.   Aux Cresson
de Volaille.   Aux Œufs.
Crôutes à la Régence.

Petits Fours Variés.
Gateaux en Variété.
Caramels de Fruits.
Biscuits Assortis.

GLACES.
Crême de Fraises.
Eau de Muscat.
Crême Caramel.
Eau de Fraises.

Café Glacé.

CHAUDS.
Thé et Café.

Searcy.   Dessert.

Menu of a winter reception.
Here is the menu of a winter wedding reception :

Consommé.

Petits Soufflés de Homard
Petits Aspics de Filets de Soles.
Médaillons de Volaille.
Aspics de Foies gras.
Croûtes à la Régence.
Tranches de Langue à la Gelée.

SANDWICHES.
de Foies gras.   de Volaille.

Petites Gelées aux fruits.
Petites Crêmes Variées.
Pâtisserie.

Biscuits Assortis.
Gâteaux Variés.

Limonade.

Macédoine de fruits.

Dessert.

Summer menu.
And this is a summer edition of the refreshments :

SANDWICHES.
Volaille.   Connaught.
Pain Bis.   de Langue.
à la Régence.   Anchois.
Aux Cresson.

Petits Fours.
Gâteaux.
Caramels de Fruits.
Biscuits Assortis.

31

The et Café.

GLACES.
Crême de Framboises.
Crême de Pain Bis.
Crême de Fraises.

Limonade.

Framboises et Crême.

Dessert.

It will be seen that the principal difference between the menus for winter and summer lies in the provision of hot soup in the former.

Champagne and claret cups frequently form part of the refreshments, and there is sometimes champagne provided for those who wish to drink to the health of bride and bridegroom.

The form, size, and character of the menu card is a matter for arrangement with the caterer from whom the refreshments are obtained. He usually supplies floral decorations as well.

The menu card.

When wedding breakfasts are given, the food is usually all cold, but sometimes hot soups are provided. The following menu is that of a smart wedding breakfast given in the month of February :

Menu of a smart wedding breakfast.

CHAUDS.
Consommé de Volaille.
Côtelettes de Mouton Panées.

WEDDING RECEPTIONS.

CHAUD-FROIDS.

Escalopes de Saumon en Mayonnaise.
Petits Paniers de Homard.
Foies gras en Caisses.
Côtelettes d'Agneau à la Connaught.
Salade Russe.
Asperges en Branches.
Tranches de Jambon.
Poulets rôtis aux Cresson.
Mirotins de Langue.
Galantine de Pigeon.

———

Sandwiches variés.

———

Bœuf épicé.
Châpon Braisé.

———

Gelées aux Liqueurs.
Bavaroise de Fruits.
Crême de Framboises.
Méringues à la Crême.
Pâtisseries.

———

GLACES.
Crême de Fraises.
Eau d'Ananas.
Eau de Muscat.

———

Dessert.

Before concluding the subject of the
entertainment of guests at weddings I
may give one more menu,
that of a breakfast where
there were five hot courses;
rather an exceptional circumstance. It was on the occasion of a
Jewish marriage, which occurred in the
month of June. The menu card was

Menu of a
Jewish wed-
ding breakfast.

bordered with a beautiful little lace
pattern embossed in silver :—

Hors d'Œuvres.

———

Consommé aux Pointes d'Asperges.
Purée de Volaille à la Celestine.

———

Saumon, sauce Tartare.
Blanchailles.

———

Tournedos à la Rossini.
Filets de Canetons aux Pois.

———

Quartier d'Agneau.
Légumes.

———

Cailles rôtis sur Croûtes.
Salade à la Venetienne.

———

Gelées aux Fraises.
Bavaroise d'Ananas
Madeleines.

———

Soufflé glacé Panaché.
Pouding à la Nesselrode.

———

Beignets de Parmesan.

———

Glaces à la Napolitaine.

———

Dessert.

FASHIONABLE WEDDINGS.

HAS any one, inexperienced in such matters, ever attempted to estimate the fatigue undergone by almost **The fatigue of the wedding week.** all concerned in the course of the week in which a wedding occurs ? Of course where great wealth enables the family of the bride to employ accomplished caterers to carry out all the details of the breakfast or reception, as the case may be, much of the cause of fatigue disappears, though by no means all. However rich the bride may be, she must try on her own clothes and supervise, in some degree, the business of packing, for never yet was maid so clever as to divine exactly what her mistress wishes to take with her on her wedding tour, and what she prefers to leave behind. And the bride **The bride's duties.** must also answer personally all notes referring to the presents she receives, and write some words of thanks, even when there is no accompanying note. It is a time of rush and hurry, in the ordinary household, and it is small wonder that those who can afford to do so entertain the wedding guests at a restaurant or at an hotel. This custom is growing so fast that it seems as if it will soon be the exception, rather than the rule, to hold the reception in one's own house when marrying a daughter.

But this will scarcely become general for the next few years, and meantime the usual method will continue to involve the usual fatigue.

The mother's part.

There are almost always relatives who expect to be asked to stay in the house for some days, if not longer, when there is a wedding in the family. If any of the bridesmaids live at a distance, it is necessary to invite them to be guests during at least three days, beginning their visit on the day before the wedding. It adds considerably to the cares of the bride's mother to have the entertainment of these young girls on her hands when her daughter has gone, unless there are other unmarried daughters left in the house. And just think of all the mother has to do in addition. Besides the additional housekeeping involved in having visitors she has to arrange all details with the caterers to whom she has entrusted the task of supplying the refreshments. It is usually the same firm that supplies the bridal cake, and they undertake the waiting as well, besides sending in everything necessary in the way of service, such as plates, dishes, glass and china, spoons, forks, knives, and table-

The guests.

The caterers.

linen, and the table or buffet itself in the case of light refreshments. The attendants are also provided by the caterers, the number of these being a matter for arrangement with the lady of the house. Her own servants will all have as much as they can manage on the wedding day, and the caterers naturally prefer that those who are in their own employ should deal with the supplies sent in. All these details fall upon the mother, and she has always some extra trouble on account of the disorganisation of the ser-

The servants. vants, who go nearly wild with excitement when there is a wedding going on. They are so anxious to be of use in every way that they incline to neglect their own special department, and the amount of chatter that goes on is something stupendous. If the mistress gets excited too, everything will go to pieces. So, however weary she may be, she must keep calm and cool, and never for an instant lose patience.

To her, too, falls the marshalling of the ceremony, the arrangements as to who shall take whom down

Arranging the ceremony. the aisle after the marriage, and who shall drive to and from the church in the different carriages. It is usual for the bride's family to have several carriages in addition to the one for the bride's use in going to church. The question of the colour of the horses is another

matter which comes up for discussion
and decision. The house-mother always finds that a number of things that
have been discussed are left to her for
final settlement. It is the experience
of every one in the onerous position of
what the Germans aptly call "Haus-
mutter"; or shall I say, "almost"
every one.

Another thing that falls to the bride
or her mother to see to is the arranging

as to the floral decorations
at the church, if there are
to be any, and also the
choice of hymns and other
music. Then there is the packing for
the journey to be seen to, for the bride
cannot always collect her thoughts
sufficiently to apply them to this
matter. With her guests to entertain, whether there is a breakfast or
only tea, and a dear daughter to part
from, there is enough for the mother to
do on the day of a wedding, is there
not?

*Church
decorations,
packing, &c.*

With reference to the choice of
horses for the occasion, at one time

a pair of greys were con-
sidered indispensable for
the bride's carriage at
least, and it was very usual for all
the carriages to have grey horses.
But that is now all changed, and it
is thought better taste to have browns
or bays. The fact is that a smart pair
of greys has been found to attract much
notice, with the consequence that an

*Colour of the
horses.*

undesirable crowd frequently assembles at the bride's house. This gathering is mainly composed of nurse-girls in charge of perambulators, and butchers' boys with material for sundry dinners of the vicinity on their wooden trays, to say nothing of fishmongers' wares, whose proximity is not always pleasant. The greys may not be responsible for all this, but they contribute largely to the circulation locally of the news. " There's a wedding at Number five " flies like wildfire round all the streets and squares. The white gloves and floral breast-knot of the coachman and footman help to spread the tale, and by the time the married couple are being pelted with rice, their collars well up to avoid the shower, every small boy in the neighbourhood, with many of its small girls, will be prepared with shafts of small wit for the occasion.

During the last few years a considerable change has occurred in the choice of bridesmaids. Formerly **Choosing the bridesmaids.** these almost invariably consisted of the sisters of the bride and bridegroom and the bosom friend of the bride. But now the bridesmaids are at least as often children as adult. They are usually the nieces of one or both of the contracting parties. There are various reasons, some of them economic, why little girls should be preferred to grown-up ones, but the change is not entirely unconnected

39

with a growing disinclination on the part of girls who are "out" to play the part of bridesmaid. Whether this has anything to do with the superstition conveyed in the old saying, "Thrice a bridesmaid never a bride," it would be difficult to decide, but certain it is that after one or two appearances in this secondary part, the average girl will be found reluctant to act in the same capacity for another friend.

In one or two instances of late the very old-fashioned plan of having groomsmen in equal num-

The revival of "groomsmen." bers with the bridesmaids has been revived. Perhaps this has been owing to the influence of the ever-increasing number of Americans among us, for the fashion obtains in the Land of the West, where the groomsmen are called ushers, and where there are far more forms and ceremonies connected with weddings than there are here. At American churches there is a procession of the bridegroom, a procession of the bridesmaids, and, last of all, the procession of the bride. This will give some idea of the elaboration of the ceremonial.

When the mother has accompanied her daughter to church, it may be supposed that she has the whole of the arrangements clearly sketched out in her mind. The left side of the church is usually reserved for the bride's relations and friends—the left side, that is, as one enters it from the principal door—and the right side for the bridegroom's friends. The reason the bride stands on the left of the bridegroom is that this betokens subjection, and it is a practical application of her coming promise to obey him ; (seldom kept !) In the vestry it is usual to ask the persons **Signing the register.** of the highest rank present to sign the register. Their signatures would follow those of the bride, bridegroom, and their fathers. It would be all settled beforehand as to what persons would be asked, as this is one of the endless matters in which it is so disastrously easy to give offence by omitting some one who might resent not being invited to append his signature. The bridegroom's mother is led down **The outgoing procession.** the church by the bride's father, or nearest relative present, the one, in short, who gave her away ; and this couple are followed by the bride's mother and the bridegroom's father. These are some of the principal things that the mother of the bride has to attend to on one of the most trying days of her life, and who shall say that a wedding in the family is not a very troublesome performance ?

The Princess of Wales's engagement ring spelt the pet name of **Engagement ring of the Princess of Wales.** the Prince. The first stone was a beryl, the second an emerald, the third a ruby, the fourth a topaz, the fifth a jacinth, and the sixth an emerald. The initial letters of the stones form the word "Bertie."

Crying is no longer fashionable. It has followed fainting into the moonlight land of half-forgotten things. It used to be in the programme of weddings that brides should weep in the vestry at least when signing their maiden name for the last time, and perhaps at the breakfast as well. But we have changed all that. Tears are now bad form. The bride who cries at her own wedding is considered to pay her bridegroom a very bad compliment.

"Tears are now bad form."

She may shed a furtive tear or two at parting from the "dearest old dad in the world," or "darling mums," but the floods of tears encouraged by the sensibility of the hot-house-bred girls of half a century ago, and kept up as an empty fashion until a few years since, have comfortably disappeared.

The modern bride is perfectly self-possessed, although she does not always imitate the coolness of the American girl who, having provided herself with a mirror by taking it to church in her carriage, got her maid to hold it up for her in the church porch, and by its aid arranged her bridal wreath and veil in full sight of the whole congregation, the waiting clergy, and the expectant choir.

The modern bride is self-possessed.

FASHIONABLE WEDDINGS.

It is now the custom for the bride-groom to completely furnish the house in which the newly-married couple intend to live. There are exceptions to every rule and sometimes the bride's father gives the whole of the furniture, but this is only when she is an heiress who marries a comparatively poor man. The ordinary rule is as stated above.

The bride-groom now furnishes the house.

The bride's only expenses are her trousseau and some wedding presents to her bridegroom. He has to give all the bridesmaids a present, as well as their bouquets. He also gives the bride her bouquet, and often gives her mother one. The bride gives presents to her pages, if she has any. Her father pays for the floral decoration of the church, the music, &c., and everything connected with the wedding day, until he bids his daughter goodbye when she leaves for the honeymoon.

The bride's expenses.

The bride's father.

MARRYING A DAUGHTER.

THE enormous increase in expenditure in every department, social and domestic, that is admittedly a feature of the century-end, is in nothing more conspicuous than weddings. Any one who can look back twenty years must be struck by the contrast. Take the item of flowers alone. The cost of a bridal bouquet varies from

The bouquets. £5 to £10, those of the bridesmaids beginning somewhere about £2, and running frequently up to £5, when such flowers as roses or carnations are chosen. This outlay falls upon the bridegroom, who has no voice in the selection of the flowers, but has merely to content himself with paying the florist's bill. The bride's parents pay the cost of the floral decorations at the church, and in the rooms where the reception is held, whether at a private house or hotel.

Even at an ordinary wedding, the reception-rooms are decorated with white flowers in a style that was unheard-of a couple of decades since. At one such, in a doctor's family, the chimney-place and fireplaces in the

Decoration of the reception-rooms.

drawing-rooms were hidden beneath a wealth of snowy blossoms, those in the grates consisting of plants in bloom, those above of cut flowers. Heat was supplied to the apartments by means of two or three wrought-iron crates filled in with cathedral glass, enclosing asbestos heated by means of oil, a highly decorative mode of heating. But think of the cost of all this! Would it not have appalled our thrifty grandmothers who contented themselves with providing a few vases of flowers for the wedding breakfast-table, and for the beautifying of the drawing-room? The great influx of Americans into English society has done much to favour the increase of expenditure on flowers. It is from them that we have borrowed the fashion of the floral wedding bell, the price of which is often most extravagant. At the wedding, not very long since, of the daughter of a well-known merchant prince, the wedding bell was composed of the most exquisite exotics, orchids, lilies, roses, gardenias, tuberoses, jessamine, and myrtle, and the hundred or so of tables at which the guests sat had each its lovely burden of snowy blooms enwreathed with smilax. The probable cost of this lavish floral decoration would be about £1,000.

American influence.

At all the best weddings real flowers are used for favours, and this is no small item when the guests number hundreds, as they usually do. Here again is a change from the old quiet ways of weddings.

Real flowers now used for favours.

When the "breakfast" was first replaced by the afternoon reception—a change that occurred soon after canonical hours for weddings were extended past noon—it was thought that a large reduction in expense would be the consequence; but it must be observed that these expectations are almost always bound to result in disappointment. Though the wedding breakfast was a very elaborate meal, with rivers of champagne and all the costly

A modern wedding tea more costly than the old "breakfast."

accompaniments inevitable, and though there is but a limited quantity of champagne consumed at a wedding tea, yet the actual expenditure on the latter is now more than was the case, as a rule, with the wedding breakfast. For every guest entertained at the latter, there are now a couple of score invited to the tea, and the caterer's services are almost invariably in request on such occasions. Five shillings per head is the usual charge for the refreshments, sometimes exclusive of ices, which form a separate item in the bill, and sometimes also apart from the flower decorations. In addition to this, a few bottles of champagne have always to be provided, in which the guests may

46

drink the health and happiness of the married pair.

Look at it all round, and on every hand a large increase of cost is only too apparent. Marrying a daughter involves as much outlay as would suffice for the household expenditure of the young couple for at least half a year. It seems all wrong; but those who desire to maintain their place in society have no choice left to them but to submit and bear the infliction as pleasantly as may be. In the matter of dress, there is also an enlarged idea, and, absurd as it seems, brides who have no prospect of being presented at Court often get married in a Court train. This is a particular which no one need imitate. The white satin dress seems to be almost necessary to the legality of the wedding ceremony, and it is worn by brides belonging to classes of society which afford no opportunity for the wearing of white satin except at the wedding.

"In the matter of dress."

The upward tendency of prices is also to be seen in the charges for carriages, especially when horsed with greys. It seems curious that these should make an increase in the price; but so it is. Ordinary pair-horse carriages are charged sixteen shillings for a wedding in the West-end of London, but a guinea is the cost of the bride's equipage with

The carriages and horses.

47

a pair of greys. At some weddings all
the carriages ordered by the parents of
the bride for the wedding have grey
horses, and this runs up the price at
the rate of about 20 per cent. The
coachmen each expect at least five
shillings as a *pour-boire*, and the
average number of carriages ordered
for a fashionable wedding is ten, so
that the cost of this portion of the
proceedings may be easily calculated.

But now we come to the wedding
cake, not one of which, even of the
most humble and inornate
character, can be obtained
for less than five guineas.
Old-fashioned hostesses who have long
since married all their daughters, and
are regarding their grandchildren as
possible brides and bridegrooms, may
remember very passable wedding cakes
in the long ago to be had at two
guineas or less, including their adorn-
ment of snowy flowers ; but now we
have changed all that, and it is not at
all unusual for the wedding cake, on
occasion, to cost forty or fifty pounds.
Some have been known to be priced at
£800, as in the case of Royal weddings, when the moulding of the
various emblematic decorations is
elaborate, and the size such as to
necessitate the use of a large van to
convey the cake from the confectioner's to the scene of the wedding
festivities. The packages in which
the various portions of the cake are

The wedding
cake.

enclosed for this transit are more suggestive of good old-fashioned Cheshire cheeses than anything else.

The stands for these wed-
Wedding cake stands. ding-cakes are in them-
selves a proof of the increased elaboration that is such a prominent and not very reassuring feature of modern fashions. These stands are sometimes composed of solid silver, but more often of fine electro-plate. The diameter is not infrequently three-quarters of a yard, and the weight of one of these with the cake superposed has been known to bring down, most ignominiously, the table on which it rested and the ceiling of the room beneath. For the ordinary wedding of the upper middle-class bride the cake usually costs from fifteen to twenty pounds, and it may be observed in passing as an indication of the eclipse of domesticity, that the cake is now usually sent out to the

friends by the confectioner,
Sending out the cake. who is merely supplied with
names and addresses by the family. Twenty or thirty years ago the bridesmaids used to meet at the parents' house the day after the wedding in order to pack the cake in the boxes prepared for it, and address them for the post; but at this end of the century domestic troubles of the sort are minimised, and we ought to be thankful, as women, that so much extra time is economised to us in this way. The

question is : What use do we make of the time thus placed at our disposal ? I very much fear we are as unthrifty with it as with many other things. What do you say, dear readers ?

The curious part of all this enforced outlay is that whereas nineteen out of every twenty mothers of marriageable daughters agree in condemning it, hardly one is to be found with sufficient courage of her opinions to resist it. It might be easy enough were it not for the consideration of the bridegroom's family, who might regard with disapprobation any efforts after a reduction of outlay. There is no doubt that the enormous expenses of modern weddings bear very hardly on the parents of many daughters, and it would be a good day when a League for the Mitigation of Outlay on Marriages should be started with the concurrence of some of those highly-placed people whose example does so much because it is seen by so many. There is no lack of sensible women among the great ones of English society, and though they insensibly go on with the current in all such matters as these, it is usually from want of having their attention directed to the possibility of their own effectual interference. Were a dozen, or a score, of influential women to give their names to any movement with a

Wanted—A League for the Mitigation of Outlay on Marriages.

Who shall start it ?

decreased rate of expenditure in social matters for its object, it would make things very much easier for the harassed and over-burdened pater-familias of the central strata of society, including the professional classes and many titled men whose income is far from being adequate to the support of a sounding handle to their names.

I have no doubt that such a move-ment would be hailed with joyful appreciation by many highly-placed individuals who recognise that things are now, and for a long time have been, drifting towards dangerous ex-cesses of outlay, necessitating a display of wealth which is not always justified, or, as the sole alternative, an open con-fession of comparative poverty. Such a dilemma is the lot of many a father and mother with regard to their daugh-ters' marriages, in the present state of things, which involves a struggle between parental love and prudence as well. Oh, for some means of simplifying the task of existence! At present everything seems to be tending to a still further stress of elaboration. Can it not be checked before it reaches a devas-tating flood-tide?

The dilemma of modern parents.

BRIDES TWO A PENNY.

In a novel recently published the supply of marriageable maidens in a country town is described as so plentiful that brides were "two a penny, like Mr. Gilbert's dukes ; while bridegrooms were like snakes in Ireland." Here is our miserable superfluity again thrown in our teeth ! It is an unfortunate circumstance that we should suffer so much from our numerosity, which, after all, is no fault of ours. In country towns the poor, dear girls outnumber the marriageable men by about six to one. At dances, picnics, cricket matches, tennis tournaments, and bicycle parades this disparity of numbers becomes peculiarly tragic. Girls who are longing to dance, the waltzes making their feet go and their whole being respond to the musical rhythm, have to sit out item after item on the programme with what patience they may collect and maintain. They must not even dance with each other, since this is always, and generally very unfairly, set down as a direct invitation to the gentlemen

"Our miserable superfluity again."

The tragedy of this disparity!

present. Oh! if they only knew how girls love dancing for itself, the fun of it, the go and whirl and mere merry motion. But young men too often imagine that the girls think more of the partners than of the dance! It is a true indictment against some of them, but not the majority by any means. It is a triumph, of course, to have plenty of partners, and not to be a wallflower for a single dance. To feel oneself " respeckit like the lave " is always agreeable ; but quite apart from that, there are thousands of girls looking forward to dances at this very moment, with pleasant expectation, that finds its sole alloy in the doubt as to whether there will be partners enough to enable them to join in every dance ; the partners being regarded as mere accessories of the pastime.

An unfair indictment.

The pretty and the rich are sure to get on well in this respect ; but, alas, for the plain girl, who has no expectations, and wears a rather shabby gown! "She should not go to dances," says some member of the censorious brigade, a company that has never to look round for recruits. This is a hard saying, good friends, whose views of life are so severe where the young people are concerned. Does not youth love fun and excitement ? And is not even the dressing and going to the ball better than nothing? And, then, you know, *one can never tell!* Magic sentence,

Alas! for the plain girl.

behind which lie such an endless series of splendid possibilities ; the printer ought to put it in golden letters.

One can never tell. Perhaps this very ball may be the turning point of the plain girl's life. Her prince may arrive upon the scene. And suppose she were to miss him by staying away ! Oh ! you may rely upon it, all the girls within miles will turn up at the ball, pretty and plain, well-dowered and poor alike, every one of them that has a chance to be there.

"One can never tell."

It is astonishing what good marriages plain girls often make. 'Tis a way they have. The pretty ones are perhaps a little spoiled. They think that to be pretty is enough. But the plain ones have often a charm of manner that induces people to look at them attentively, and discover many a good point, which has the attraction of the unexpected. Few people realise how subtle is this fascination. The recognised beauty dazzles indeed. She takes beholders by storm. " How lovely she is ! " says the newly-introduced, and the social lustre shed by her upon the men whom she allows to be in her company is at once recognised. But there is, to many men, a peculiar pleasure in discovering for themselves the charm of girls whose good looks are not universally appreciated, or even acknowledged. There are

The charm of the plain girl.

Beauty not for the crowd.

forms of beauty which do not appeal to the crowd. Some of the loveliest women in England did not develop their attractiveness until they were twenty-five or thereabouts. I could name three or four of whom this has been conspicuously true. Sometimes it is an even chance whether a girl of eighteen may turn out a beauty or a failure in the matter of looks. Let no plain girls despair !

If only there were not such an over-supply ! It is a disheartening circumstance to the young and gay. *The gist of the matter.* And it is so very bad for men to feel themselves in so much demand. They think it is owing to their intrinsic qualities that they are so well appreciated, asked out everywhere and made much of. But the gist of the matter lies in the often-heard sentence :

" Young men are so scarce ! "

Were the cases suddenly altered, and girls to become scarce, with bride-grooms two a penny, what *But if the cases were reversed!* a mortifying change would result for many a young man who now feels a conviction that he possesses every desirable qualification. He would soon find his level, that young man ! and very astonishing would be some of his discoveries. It would be very good for him. It is probably owing to his comparative scarcity that the young man of the present day goes up to

a girl in a ball-room and says, "Would
you like to dance this waltz?" instead
of the more polite, "May I have the
pleasure of this waltz?" or, "Will you
give me a dance?" I have even known
instances where the familiar "Come
along" has been considered sufficient
invitation. And the girl was only too
glad to go, knowing that it was her
only chance of dancing. With brides
at two a penny, what else could be
expected?

In Roman Catholic countries the
matter is simplified by the number of
girls who enter convents, but
here in England we neither
have, nor wish for, any such
method of reducing the disparity of
numbers. Nor does emigration appeal
very strongly to the girls of middle-
class families. A visit to friends in
India has furnished many with a chance
of "settling" that seemed far enough
away at home. But the old idea that
a woman who remains unmarried is a
social failure has long been obsolete.
Some of the most popular members of
London Society are to be found among
its spinsters. Sneers about "unappro-
priated blessings" are much
less frequent among the
cultured classes. They are
relegated to a lower stratum, where
good breeding and open-mindedness
are not particularly common qualities.
Jeers about "old maids" become more
and more infrequent. They were

Some remedies.

And more rational ideas.

horribly unjust. Many an unmarried woman has refused half a dozen suitors for no worse reason than that her standard of manliness has always been a high one, so high that none of the men she has ever met have approached it. Is there any shame in this? Not to fall to her share, most certainly, though in the servants' hall she may be regarded with a superb scorn in consequence.

In the very unbalanced state of things, the supply of husbands being so insufficient, it is not surprising that girls grumble a little over the inveterate habit indulged in by widows of marrying again. But it is hopeless to try to cure them of it! They will insist on being charming. They are often younger in mind and spirit, as well as more youthful in looks, than their unmarried contemporaries, and they have always such unimpeachable, logical reasons for marrying again. If their first choice was an unhappy one, is not that an excellent argument for trying again to find a woman's highest earthly bliss, a home where love, joy and peace may continually reign? If, on the other hand, she passed some pleasant years with her first husband, she feels so sadly lonely after losing him that she marries again in an endeavour to recover the sense of companionship. So, which ever way one takes the

The incorrigible widow.

Whose logic is unassailable.

widow, her position is impregnable.
Her only weak point, her

Her only weak point. Achilles heel, is that she is
for ever excusing herself for
her second venture, and there never
was a truer proverb than that which
tells us that *"Qui s'excuse, s'accuse."*

Perhaps the accusations of her unmarried friends suggest the excuses!
She is sure to be gently scolded by
them for appropriating two husbands
when there are not enough to go round.
It does seem rather selfish. But girls,
nowadays, are not brought

Nowadays one is first a woman. up with a single eye to
matrimony, as they used to
be. At this end of the
century one is first a woman, then a
possible wife. There is one's own life
to be lived, apart from the partnership
that may be entered into by and by.
The idea used to be that it was a wife's
duty to sink her individuality completely, and live only for her husband ;
to spend her whole time, in fact, in
carrying out her part of the marriage
contract. The contented spinster may
well say to herself, as she regards some
of the husbands to whom her friends
have mated themselves :

" Had I married the Tommies—oh, Lord !
　To loove an' obaäy the Tommies !
　　I couldn't 'a stuck by my word."

A man of mediocrity has his own
ideal of a wife. The sort he likes is
one who dresses handsomely and be-

comingly on a very small allowance.
She must never go into
debt for anything, but must
always pay ready - money,
whether she can manage to
get it from him or not. Her jewels must
on no account be eclipsed by those of
other women of her set, but when she
buys them, and the bill comes in, her
husband is furious about the outlay.
He sulks for a week, but then he would
have sulked quite as long if, at the last
dinner-party, she had shone a secondary
star to any lady of their acquaintance.
A man loves his wife to be gentle and
sympathetic to himself. If
she is too much so to her
boys, and they take advantage of it and get into debt
and go to her to help them out, then
he says, " Bother sympathy." If she
is too good to the poor, and gives
them of the household abundance, he
is apt to be cynical and censorious :
talks of "encouraging a parcel of idle
rogues," of "indiscriminate charity,"
and the harm it does and of the danger
of pauperising the needy. None of
these considerations, however, prevent
him from giving to charities that print
his name at the head of subscription
lists, or forking out a shilling for cases
that come under his immediate notice.
It is only the wife who is to subordinate her kindly impulses to considerations of political economy. A man
likes his wife to be cheerful. He does

She must shine on nothing a-year.

Be sympathetic so long as his pocket is not touched.

not always concern himself very particularly about the means to
Cheerful, though he cuts her to the quick. make and keep her so, but
he disapproves utterly of
a sad or pensive face. He
may have cut her to the quick with
some bitter word before he leaves
home in the morning, but he is excessively annoyed if he perceives on re-
turning any signs of the wound he has
inflicted. As Mrs. Fraser said in "The
Benefit of the Doubt," "A man hits
hard, but he never expects to see a
bruise." He has forgiven himself for
administering the blow, why should not
the recipient be equally quick about
it? A man likes his wife to be intelligent, quite sufficiently so to be able to
conduct the concerns of life, and to
appreciate his own intellectual parts
and enjoy stray ebullitions of
And intellectual, though not to fathom his shallowness. his wit and humour. She
must applaud these with
discrimination, and in that
delicate manner which in-
fers no surprise at his possessing
brilliancy. But he is exasperated if
she should be too intelligent. He does
not like to be divined. His depths are
to be inviolate ; but he likes to sound
her shallows ; and so well does she
know this that she often assumes a
shallowness when she has it not.

Are these little hints of any use ?

ETHICS OF DRESS.

WOMEN dress irrationally. I admit it fully and completely. And though **The irrationality of women's dress.** men—yes, men—have lectured about the irrationality of our dress, I can assure them that for every point they bring against it I could tell them four or five more. No one knows so well as women themselves how very inconvenient modern dress is. The only time that we don't grumble about it is when we see a sister-woman attired in "rational" costume. It is then **When we cease to grumble.** that we hug our faults and follies to our breasts, and delight in our delinquencies. We compare those heel-less prunella shoes with our own neat patents—wicked things they are, though, with their pointed toes and narrow soles. We contrast their shapeless figures with our own smart outlines, and are so lost to a sense of **The punishment for our sins.** our sartorial sins as to congratulate ourselves on our sumptuary superiority. The mood does not last long. We soon begin again to feel where the shoe pinches—perhaps the corset, too—to suffer from the weight of over-wide skirts, and to commiserate ourselves for difficulties with hats and hairpins. How truly fiendish a hairpin can be no mere man can ever know. When it presses against the skull and produces a local nerve-torture of an indescribably vicious nature, a man might imagine that the easy thing would be to pull it out. Only the rashest of women would venture upon such a course of action. Like Hamlet, we prefer to bear those ills we have than fly to others that we know not of. For if, in the withdrawal of that single pin, the whole bright coiffure should come tumbling down, ay! there's the rub! A woman feels so tremendously at a disadvantage if her hair is untidy. She cannot even argue till it is neat again!

That fiendish hairpin!

And why do women dress irrationally? Well, in strictest confidence, I can give several good reasons. If we did not do so, we should be unpleasantly singular. The men who belong to us would call us dowdy, and would shirk escorting us to our pet restaurants, our favourite theatres, and even to church. Men are like that. They are really more sensitive to public opinion than women. That is why they always give a cabman more than his fare. A man likes the women of his household to be smart and up-to-date in

Some reasons for our irrational dress.

The cowardice of the men-folk.

dress and appearance. He can say, "What *have* you got on?" in an awful voice, a blend of scorn and disapproval that strikes inward like mismanaged measles. "Oh, it's my new gown," says the palpitating victim, trying to be airy and at her ease. "Your *what?*" And then follows a colloquy that can be left to the imagination, marital manners not being always improving to the mind. Here, then, is one reason why we dress in an inconvenient and often unhygienic way. Another is that it is extremely expensive to wear clothes that are different from those of the ordinary kind. If one wants an out-of-the-way gown or bonnet, one has to give both time and money to the getting of it. Dressmakers, too, object to making anything in which their customers look like "guys." It does them no credit and brings them no *kudos*, consequently they charge more for the work, and are never in a good temper when trying the garment on the strongminded wearer.

The question of cost.

Tyranny of the dressmaker.

And yet another good reason for abstaining from the singular in dress is that the quality is an infectious one. An eccentric costume nourishes and developes eccentricity in the wearer. After having been hardened by a few remarks from street-boys, and having discovered herself to be the

And the infectious nature of eccentricity.

63

subject of public comment among omnibus drivers and cabbies on various occasions, the " rational " dresser finds peculiarities cropping up in her mode of thought and budding into those " little ways," those curious habits which do so much to avert sympathy and even affection from the person who contracts them. Let us, then, be irrational with the rest of the world, for awhile. We were not created for wearing clothes, and we shall probably, in any event, never make a success of it.

The object of a fashionable woman in dressing, is to make herself distinctive without becoming conspicuous—to excel by her union of graceful outline and fidelity to the fashion of the moment (no easy task), and, while offering no striking contrast to those around her, so to individualise herself that she is one of the few who remain in the memory, when the crowd of well-dressed women is recalled only as an indistinguishable mass. There are half a dozen women in London society who succeed in thus accomplishing a task that bristles with contradictions.

The object of fashionable dress.

When the number of necessary details are considered, the wonder is that there are so many brilliant successes. As things are, many fail in such trifles as fastening on a veil, adjusting the collar or the ribbons at neck and waist, or in achieving the necessary harmony between costume and coiffure. And no one, not even the most expert, is invariably successful ; but then the triumphs are all the more brilliantly effective by reason of an occasional failure.

There is intense vulgarity in dressing in loud colours and glaring styles in order to attract attention to oneself. There is an immense difference between this sort of thing and the desire to look one's best, and to be as becomingly and suitably attired as one's means allow. To make the most of one's appearance and do credit to one's friends are legitimate objects at which to aim in the art of dress.

AT fashionable restaurants evening dress is the rule at the dinner hour.

Evening dress the rule. I have seen ladies turned back at Prince's Restaurant because they had hats on and declined to remove them. Those who are going on to opera or dance wear full dress at these dinners.

AT WEDDINGS.

THE bride's white satin is now often replaced by silk muslin, chiffon or lace.

White satin not essential. Should she elect to be married in travelling dress, her bridesmaids wear smart visiting costumes instead of the usual white or light-tinted bridemaidenly attire.

Dress of a bride if a widow. A widow, when marrying again, wears grey, mauve, heliotrope, lavender, biscuit or deep cream-colour, or any tint not mournful or lugubrious. She has no bridesmaids but is usually accompanied by one "maid of honour" whose dress must not be so light of hue as to eclipse her own.

DRESS on the river partakes of the
nature of seaside costume, but is usually
less rigorously tailor-cut.
More ornament is permitted
than in the case of yachting
dress, but lace-trimmed
white petticoats and black patent
shoes are equally out of place for
both, suiting not the nature of a boat.

An amount of ornamentation allowable.

TRAVELLING DRESS.

TRAVELLING costumes consist of tweed,
serge, Irish frieze, home-
spun, and other all-wool
materials, and are of the
class of tailor-mades.

Should be tailor-made.

In hot weather white muslins, piqués
and flowered or pale muslins are worn
by the sea, with open-
worked white stockings
and white shoes. Alpacas,
surahs, foulards, and mohairs are suitable for seaside and travelling dress.
To wear satin, brocade or rich heavy
silks is as great a solecism
as for a man to don frock-
coat and silk hat at seaside
places or when travelling.
Glittering bead trimmings and elaborate
embroideries are also quite out of place,
and should be reserved for more ceremonious occasions.

In hot weather.

Some solecisms in dress.

SEASIDE AND COUNTRY DRESS.

FOR seaside and country wear tailor-made costumes are indispensable, **Tailor-mades indispensable.** the materials being cloth, serge, homespun and other woollens. But this rule does not apply to fashionable **At race-meets, garden-party dress.** race-meetings, such as Sandown, Ascot, Epsom, Goodwood, &c., where garden-party dress is usually seen, though tailor-mades are by no means out of place, when smartly built and accompanied by something rather ornate in the way of headgear.

Without entering upon any details of present fashions, which would probably be out-of-date before this **A summary.** book is even published, I may perhaps summarize the principal rules of good society on the **Morning dress.** subject. In the morning, the toilette should be comparatively simple, even in town during the season. In the after- **For afternoons.** noon a certain amount of elaboration — more or less according to circumstances—is usually imported into the costume. **Evening dress.** Evening dress includes two styles, full and demi-toilette. The former exacts uncovered arms and shoulders ; the latter admits of partially covering both. The former comprises ball and dinner dress. The latter suffices for the theatre. Full dress is worn in private boxes and stalls at the opera, but it is only the ladies of the upper middle-class who wear full dress at the theatres.

Ball, dinner and opera dress.

The Princess of Wales and her daughters favour a less *décolleté* style. Ladies of high rank who sit in the stalls usually keep on their mantles, which are of a sort adapted to the season and the draughty character of many theatres.

For theatres— the demi-toilette.

BICYCLING COSTUME.

THE usual tailor-made, cut considerably shorter in the skirt and arranged with due consideration of the exigencies of wheeling, constitutes the ordinary bicycling dress, with a neatly-cut coat and a hat not over-trimmed. The regular bicycling costume is not unlike a shooting suit, for details of which, as well as of fishing costumes, I may refer readers to their favourite tailor. And with regard to riding habits and jackets I have also but little to say, as those who can afford to indulge in these pastimes are at no loss for the advice of the best firms, and are therefore independent of anything to be culled from books.

Tailor-made, cut short in the skirt.

Riding habits and jackets.

DINNERS AND DINNER PARTIES.

THE hostess who gives good dinners is pretty sure to succeed in social life, and will be almost certain to marry her daughters well. *Qualities of a good hostess.* There are many more admirable qualities than those that go to make up the excellent housekeeper, but there are none more popular, in their result. Nor are these qualities either common or to be despised. Let us reckon them up. First must come that amiability that is desirous of pleasing. *The desire to please.* Many a fairly successful hostess is destitute of this, but it is chiefly in such cases where her position is high and her social influence consequently great. In the ordinary walks of life no one is likely to cultivate a rude woman, and it is for hostesses in the ordinary walks of life that this little volume is intended.

The next item in the equipment of a good hostess is tact, a quality about which whole books have *Tact.* been written and yet which has never been satisfactorily defined. The fact is, it is—

" Like the milky way i' the sky,
    A meeting of gentle lights without a name."

Tact is both innate and acquired. The root of the thing must be born with the possessor, or the soil will prove uncongenial. Years of mingling in good society are necessary to its full development, and though a delicate sense of what is due to others is of the very essence of tact, it is never quite perfect without a knowledge of the gentle art of snubbing. This is an accomplishment which some women never acquire. They cannot firmly repress the unduly officious or the over-eager without adopting harsh measures or losing their temper. Where they should simply ignore, they administer the cut direct. When a phrase, well sharpened and skilfully aimed, would answer all purposes, even if uttered with the gentlest voice and with the politest intonation, they avail themselves of weapons that should not be found in any gentlewoman's armoury. The "retort courteous" loses none of its point for being courteous, and how agreeably it compares with the bludgeon style of warfare of some fair warriors!

The gentle art of snubbing.

But the woman who cannot snub, on occasion, may be pronounced almost incapable of giving good dinners. Her visiting list, instead of being kept carefully weeded, will certainly run to seed in a way that will militate against the harmonious selection of her guests.

A third necessary qualification for the part of hostess is the possession of a

palate. We cannot all afford to employ cooks so unimpeachable
A well-trained palate. that everything they turn
out is absolutely perfect, and
even if we could they would soon grow
careless in the employ of a mistress
who could not sufficiently discriminate
to award praise or blame—the latter in
very minute doses, of course. Men say
that women have no palate, in the sense
of accurately discerning
Able to appreciate and discriminate. flavours and distinguishing
between those that have
some points of similarity.
Is the accusation true? If not, why
are the best and cleverest cooks all
men? And why do *chefs* and *cordon
rouges* invariably prefer to serve a man
rather than a woman? But, be this
as it may, the perfect hostess must
be one of the exceptionally endowed
(I yield the point for lack of data), and
capable of appreciating down to the
smallest detail the culinary efforts of
her cook.

Good taste is another essential point,
for though it is now possible
General good taste. to leave much of the minu-
tiæ of dinner-giving in the
hands of caterers and others, there are
details that must rest with the hostess
herself. Take the choice of plates and
dishes, for instance. Perhaps we hardly
realise how much our en-
The dinner service. joyment of a meal depends
on the character of the
immediate accompaniments. The most

accomplished gourmets prefer the simplest plates, and the fashion has for several years ruled in consonance with this idea. The favourite plates are white or cream-coloured with a narrow margin or slender line of colour, and sometimes the crest or monogram—or the crest *and* monogram—of the owner in a circle or medallion at the side. Dishes matter less, since they are rarely seen on the table nowadays, but those on the sideboard will be naturally of the same pattern as the plates. The taste of the hostess will also be displayed in the floral decora-

Table decorations. tions, for though these are often left to the caterer, and can usually be safely left to him, yet his efforts are subordinate to the arrangements he has made in consultation with the lady who employs him.

A common fault in table decoration is to over-do it. Half a dozen great bowls of roses down the

Simplicity most effective. centre of the table are rather overpowering, and the effect is much better when comparatively few flowers are used and a light and graceful effect is aimed at. The form of the vases is an important item, and the idea that none but costly things can

Costly vases not needed. please has been long exploded. Some of the prettiest vases are the cheapest, and lovely as exotics are, they may often with advantage be replaced by inexpensive blooms which are better able

74

to withstand the heat of the room and the hot odours of the dishes. What can exceed, for instance, the beauty of the Iceland poppy, which one can procure in June and July at a low price? And in August, September and October there is the lovely Cape gooseberry, with its tiny balloons of gold and orange and crimson. And I have seen a table look beautiful with nothing more elaborate than sprays of silver honesty rising out of banks of scarlet geranium. There can hardly be a less costly decoration than this, but the effect of table decoration is often excellent in inverse ratio to its cost.

Nor costly flowers.

We are always being told that table-centres are going out of fashion, but it is doubtful if they will ever completely do so. They afford the best means of filling the vacancy left by the absent dinner dishes and the huge and heavy épergne that, once on a time, occupied the middle. With five or six centres in different pale tints, one can endlessly vary one's effects, and if the available vases are such as will match or contrast with these effectively, a great point will be gained. The centres may be pale green, rose-pink, pure white, orange and poppy-coloured, and the choice among them must be regulated by the flowers procurable. A most lovely autumn decoration can be made with

Table-centres.

A lovely autumn decoration.

an orange centre and the carefully sponged leaves of golden bracken, a few pale lemon-coloured nasturtiums and a little maidenhair mingled with them. The bracken, fern and nasturtiums would also look lovely on palest green satin or bright, soft, sky-blue. The fashion of strewing flowers upon the cloth has not the suffrages of the flower-lover. It is disagreeable to such to see the blossoms wither. Smilax, which is so difficult to grow, seems To preserve smilax. to be particularly retentive of vitality, and may with impunity be hung from candelabra or laid upon the cloth. It will not suffer, and will last for two or three dinners if completely submerged in cold water all night and gently shaken and dried the next morning.

Wild flowers have a poetic sound in association with the dinner-table, but they are not always an Wild flowers. artistic success. They droop too quickly, " get sleepy," as children describe it, and shut up their pretty petals in a way that gives them a forlorn appearance, and makes the table look positively squalid. Autumn leaves can be preserved for table To preserve autumn leaves. decoration when they have put on their fullest tint of gold or red, of russet or tan, by softly sponging them with the least possible moisture on the sponge and then ironing them with a tepid iron, after-wards painting them over with a weak solution of gum. If they are then laid out to dry, and carefully protected from wet or gusty airs, they will in a day or two be ready to put away under a weight, being first folded in a soft linen cloth.

In nothing more than in the exquisite glass have we changed the aspect of our dinner-tables since the days when plain white damask, of the thickest and finest, it is true, was the only resource of the dainty housewife. The strip of daintily-tinted brocade down the centre of the table, or the waves and ripples of pale pink, mauve, yellow, or sky-blue silk, give a relief to the white, which is invaluable from an artistic point of view. A novel and pretty dinner-table was recently arranged with folds of printed Indian silk in scarlet and yellow, loosely disposed in waves up the centre of the table. On this stood one large and two smaller glass vases decorated with designs in gold, and filled with scarlet and yellow tulips and asparagus tops, lovely lines of smilax running all round in and out among the vases, and outlining the edges of the Indian silk down the sides of the table. Here and there a single tulip was placed among the folds, with its grey-green leaves looking as though it were growing.

Coloured silk reliefs.

A novel arrangement.

What should we do without the chrysanthemum in our long winters when flowers are very dear? The

blossoms seem to grow more beautiful with every year that passes ;
The chrysan-themum as a table flower. and their enormous variety of tint also seems to be increasing. There are the yellow flowers, the shade of which is in the brightest and most cheerful tone, the one which always makes me think of the Chinese name for yellow, "the daughter of light." Even in the day-light these lovely flowers suggest sun-shine when there is, alas ! not one scrap of it about. Then there are the deep crimson chrysanthemums, the edges of the petals just touched with fawn. These light up most exquisitely. They require the relief of maidenhair or some light leaf, such as as-
Asparagus-tops as reliefs. paragus-tops, to which we owe such a debt of gratitude for their graceful abundance. Pure white chrysanthemums seem to grow to a larger size than coloured. Some of them emulate cheese-plates—or what once were known as such—in extent. Their thousand petals have each a different form. It is worth examining one of these to note the extraordinary variety. Not even two are edged alike, and the effect of the lovely flowers is enormously enhanced by this infinite difference. But lovely as they are, they
Coloured flowers are best for the table. do not tend so well to deco-rate the dinner-table as coloured flowers and those of smaller size. Contrast with the snowy cloth is necessary, and,

in order to produce this, pure white flowers have to be combined with scarlet or orange or bright pink, such as tulips and red geraniums, the brilliant plumes of the begonia, the lovely flowers of the nasturtium, which, not everybody knows, can be cultivated in our rooms throughout the winter, in water, like hyacinths and tulips ; or the berries of the solanum, which are so attractive in their variety of scarlet, orange, and gold.

The lovely Nice roses, with their mellow cream colour heightened with dainty pink edges, and their green leaves lined with brown, make a dinner-table look not only beautiful, but refined. It might be imagined that every flower imparts this aspect of refinement ; but, strange as it seems, it is not always so. The art of the florists has now won for us such concessions from nature as permit us to rejoice in abundance of lovely flowers which once we could only obtain during a few weeks of every year. The lily of the valley, for instance ; the violet, which is always with us ; the rose, the orchid, the tulip, and the white and mauve lilac. To this list may be added the lovely cyclamen which brightens our homes all through the gloomy winter, and has a hidden vigour which needs only care and encouragement to preserve the frail-looking rose-tinted stems and keep them in condition for many weeks.

The Nice rose adds refinement.

The cyclamen.

The fashion of the moment is for mauve and heliotrope, and at a dinner-table at Prince's, the centre was embellished with a bank of heliotrope silk muslin printed in gold, in which were set cream and gold vases filled with pale Nice roses. The contrast of colour was quite up-to-date and very effective.

A very dainty table has a band of broad open lace insertion running up on either side just beyond the level of the diners' plates. Within this is a border of green moss, outlining a rippling sea of yellowish cream-coloured brocade, the gold threads of which glint in the electric light that falls, softly shaded to the eyes of the diners, from above. The brocade is in a design of gold thistle leaves, on a ground of creamy white. From the centre rises a tall, trumpet-shaped vase of palest green, holding aloft tall sprays of creamy orchids with delicate touches of brown and gold upon the lips. The stem of the vase is wreathed with smilax, and similar vases alternate with gold candelabra down the centre of the table. So pretty was the effect of this that it was photographed, and the fact of the portrait of it lying before me accounts for my writing of it in the present tense.

I never like to see slippers as flower-vases on the dinner-table. The associations of shoes and food is not an agreeable idea ; and there is

Slippers as flower-vases. also an old superstition against placing boots or shoes upon a table. It is a mistake to put before any guest what may make him uncomfortable in relation to any superstition he may have cherished ; and is there one of us who has not some weak point in this connection ?

A pretty table at a winter dinner. Down the centre of a pretty table was a drift of rose-pink and silver gauze, in itself a delicious bit of colour and texture. It was bordered with long trails of smilax which passed under miniature arches of holly and mistletoe. In the centre of the table rose a small ivy tree, hung on all the branches with peals of tiny silver bells, which tinkled with fairy music at every movement of the guests. Trails of smilax hung from candelabra to candelabra, all down the table, tied with pink ribbon, and the candles were shaded with pink. The small vases at the corners were filled with pink roses and brown ivy, and at the plate of each diner lay a " buttonhole," consisting of a rose and an ivy spray. Pink-shaded lamps and baskets of flowers, chiefly pink tulips, palms and ferns, tied up with pink ribbons, and wreathed with smilax round the tall handles, stood on the sideboard and on the writing-table and at other points of vantage through the room.

One of the newest and prettiest ways of decorating the dinner-table is by hanging a basket from the **The hanging basket.** ring in the ceiling to which the now almost obsolete gas-chandelier once used to be attached. From this basket depend long trails of smilax, ivy (brown and green) with each leaf polished to a high perfection of glossiness. The conservatory sometimes yields, even in autumn, long fronds of the humble but decorative creeping-jenny. Any rusty leaves must be carefully cut away, or the effect will be wholly spoiled.

Flowers are a fascinating subject but must not be allowed to occupy an undue proportion of our space.

Among the dainty etceteras of the tables the menu holders and menu cards repay some care and **Menu holders and cards.** taste, and the delicately tooled silver dishes in pierced work for bonbons are seen on every well-laid table when a dinner party is in question. It is in matters like these that the taste of the hostess is clearly shown.

THE INVITATIONS.

THE usual length of invitation for a dinner party is three weeks, but this is by no means a fixed rule. **The length of invitations.** In the height of the London season it may be abridged or extended, according to circumstances. Sometimes a hastily got up dinner is given for some one who is passing through London, or visiting some provincial town. Perhaps it may be some celebrity to be invited to meet whom is regarded as a great honour. Foolish indeed, and inexperienced in the ways of the great world, would be the person who would take exception to a short invitation in these circumstances. In the same way a distant date is sometimes fixed at a time when every one may be supposed to be fully engaged for weeks to come, and a dinner invitation has been received as much as six weeks in advance of the date fixed. This is, of course, very exceptional.

There are two forms of invitation; the purely formal, and the "friendly" as it may be almost officially **Forms of invitation.** called. The former is usually written on an invitation card, but not invariably so, while the latter is written on note paper of the small size known to stationers as "invitation note." The card is worded as follows :

<table>
<tr><td>The formal invitation</td><td>MR. and MRS. BROWN
request the pleasure of
MR. and MRS. GREEN'S
company to Dinner
on Tuesday, July 9th, at 8 o'clock.
R.S.V.P.</td></tr>
</table>

The friendly note usually runs as follows :

The friendly note. "Dear Mrs. Green,—Will you and Mr. Green give us the pleasure of your company at dinner on Tuesday, July 9th, at eight o'clock ? "

or :

" Dear Mrs. Green,—Will you and Mr. Green dine with us in a friendly way on Tuesday, July 9th, at eight o'clock ? "

The mode of replying is regulated by that of the invitation. It would be a great mistake to answer a friendly note with a formal one, and though not nearly so heinous a crime, replying to a formal card by a note in the first person is sometimes misunderstood. If there are circumstances to be explained as to why the invitation cannot be accepted, it is sometimes well to write in the first person, but this only applies in particular instances. A short explanation can very well be couched in the third person.

" Mrs. Black regrets very much that

she is unable to accept Mrs. Grey's kind invitation for the 9th as she will not be in town, having arranged to spend a fortnight with some friends in Lincolnshire."

The formula " Owing to a previous engagement " has been so often used to convey studied incivility that a reason for declining an invitation has now come to be considered almost a necessity, except in the most formal cases, or where the acquaintanceship is very slight.

The reason for declining should be given.

It is related of Lord Charles Beresford that, on one occasion, when invited to dine at Marlborough House, he wired the following reply : " Sorry to be unable to accept. Lie follows by post." This anecdote may possibly be true, but it seems most improbable, and for more reasons than one.

However, it is certainly true that many a little fib is told in such cases, and if it were only true that the end justifies the means, some of them would be harmless enough. The ones that are devised with the object of sparing pain to the recipient ought surely to rank in a very different category from those that are inspired by envy, hatred, malice and all uncharitableness.

The kindly fib.

INVITATION CARDS.

THE form of invitation cards varies slightly, but the simplest are *The best people use the simplest card.* those used by persons of the highest rank. The usual size is 4½ by 3½ inches, and the printed characters are copper-plate. The lines run as follows :

MR. and MRS. BLANK
request the pleasure of

———————————————————————

Company at Dinner

on ——————————————————————

—— o'clock.

56, Highland Square.   R.S.V.P.

It will be seen that the only items to be filled in are the name or names of the guests, the date, and hour. Sometimes the word " honour " is used instead of " pleasure," and occasionally the " R.S.V.P." is replaced by " An answer will oblige," an ungrammatical sentence which some persons prefer to the initial letters of the French phrase. It is improved upon in " An answer is requested." Those who do not care to copy the customs of the *Crests.* aristocracy often have their crests in gilding on their invitation cards, and I have even seen two crests ornamenting one card.

THE MENU AND WINES.

It is scarcely necessary to remark that it is a sad failure in good manners to neglect any point concerning the comfort and enjoyment of one's guests. "To invite people to one's house," says Brillat Savarin, "is to charge oneself with their happiness so long as they remain in it." What can one think of the host who offers his friends indifferent wine? George Meredith, in "The House on the Beach," describes in his own forcible language the results of drinking some men's wine :—

A hostess charges herself with the comfort of her guests.

Indifferent wines.

"A sip of his wine fetched the breath as when men are in the presence of the tremendous elements of nature. It sounded the constitution more darkly-awful, and with a profounder testimony to stubborn health, than the physician's instruments."

Champagne and all white wines should be served cold, but the temperature should be lowered in bottle, not in the glass. To cool champagne properly lay the bottle down

To cool champagne.

in a basin, break up a handful of ice, put it on the bottle, sprinkle it with a little salt, and cover it with a wet piece of flannel. Do this two hours before you serve the wine, and the result will be most gratifying.

To moderately cool Sauterne and Rhine wines brings out their bouquet and gives them an agreeable, fresh, spicy taste. Claret and Burgundy, on the contrary, should be drunk milk - warm. This condition is secured by carefully setting the bottle in hot water, and allowing it to remain long enough to gently heat the wine. This brings out its body and diminishes any tendency to astringency.

Claret and Burgundy should be milk-warm.

Port and sherry lose in body and flavour by being chilled. Port through exposure to cold acquires a harsh, thin, acid taste, often akin to bitterness, and is temporally defrauded of all its characteristic qualities. Sherry and Madeira apparently lose their body, become thin, hide their rich, mellow oiliness, and have none of the nutty flavour which properly belongs to them.

Port and sherry should not be chilled.

That the food offered is the best of its kind should equally be the care of the hostess. It is quite unnecessary to have things that are out of season, and consequently expensive. The dishes may be plain and

The food should be the best of its kind.

simple, but, whatever they are, they should be the best sort procurable, and cooked with the best skill that the hostess can command. It is a poor compliment to ask a number of people to sit down to an ill-prepared repast. But very few are guilty of this. In fact, the error is usually that of the other extreme, viz., trying to do more than is justified by the finances or resources of the giver of the feast. The result is, that the hostess is a wearied, worn-out being when she sits down to dinner, incapable from over-fatigue of guiding the conversation or of preserving that equanimity that keeps her

And the cooking the best in one's power.

One should avoid the other extreme.

" Mistress of herself though china fall."

The subject of menus for dinner is too vast a one to be treated here. Suffice it to say that the home-cooking can often be supplemented by a soup and an *entrée* or sweet dish from a caterer's — an excellent way of reducing the cook's task and of introducing something fresh and novel without very great trouble or expense.

Supplementing the home-cooking.

In " Manners for Men " I have gone into so much detail on the subject of the dinner-party from start to finish, that I should only be repeating myself were I to enter on the subject here with any fulness. All I need add to the matter contained in some thirty pages of the little volume is to remind dinner guests of my own sex that either full or demi-toilette is necessary, and that the gloves are kept on till the wearer seats herself at table. They may or may not be resumed after dinner, though usually the right-hand glove is put on previous to hand-shakings and goodbyes before the party breaks up. At very formal houses, where the hostess is a dragon of social etiquette, one dares not relax the smallest rule. But it is usually among those of highest rank that such observances are least regarded.

The toilette of guests.

Resuming gloves after dinner.

The hostess must shake hands with all her guests, whether her previous acquaintance with them has been slight or the reverse. They are her guests, and she is bound to give them the welcome of a hand-shake, even if she never saw or heard of them before. The sole exception is that of royalty, and in this case the hostess waits for her guest to hold out his or her hand. The question of precedence is always a difficult one, and more so, in one way, in middle-class society than in higher circles where there are

The hostess shakes hands with all her guests.

Except when they are of the Royal Family.

regular degrees of rank. All this must be arranged beforehand, and the places at table settled. Sometimes name-cards are used, and this is a very convenient custom. That it is not followed in the highest society need not prevent the ordinary hostess from availing herself of a plan that averts many difficulties. Failing the name-cards, the host, who enters the dining-room first with the lady of highest social status, must be fully instructed as to the position of the guests, and the butler should also be told where each couple is to sit. But, of course, this is useless if the people are all unknown to him. He cannot be expected to keep in his mind the names of a number of people, even though he has just announced them in the drawing-room on their arrival.

The question of precedence.

The hostess goes last of all into the dining-room with the gentleman of most importance present— that is, of most importance socially. The signal to leave the table is given in the merest nod or smile to the lady who had been taken down by the host. She is sure to be on the look-out for it ; but if she is not, it is sufficient to rise, whereupon all the ladies get up at once. It is well, however, to make a decided effort to catch the eye of the principal lady, as she might consider it a slight if the hostess were to make

The hostess enters the dining-room last.

Departure of the ladies.

the move without the usual co-operation. It might, besides, be set down to ignorance. In choosing the moment for this move, it is usual to take three or four things into consideration. Time must be allowed for the discussion of the dessert, and every one must have quite finished before the signal is given. But it must not be made at the very moment that some one has just laid down a knife or fork or a wine-glass, lest it might appear that the whole party had been waiting for the conclusion of that one individual's meal. If any one is in the midst of an animated or interesting conversation, the move must be deferred until it slackens off a little. On the other hand, should any disagreeable or unwelcome topic arise, the signal is sometimes prematurely given, in order to make a diversion. The ladies leave the dining-room in the same order in which they entered it; first, the lady of highest rank, and the hostess last.

Points for consideration in giving the signal.

There has been a curious revulsion of late against the slow and tedious two or three hours' dinner party. The Prince of Wales was the first to suggest and have practically carried out in his own family the shorter dinner with fewer courses. But now the tendency is rather too much in the opposite direction.

The revulsion against too long dinners.

A writer in a French paper makes

strong protest against the excessive
rapidity with which the
courses follow each other
at table. It is a reaction
against the wearisome slow-

The tendency
to go to
the other
extreme.

ness of the old style, and, like almost
all reactionary influences, it has a tendency to rush to the other extreme.
The writer in question pleads for time
to eat and talk, not merely to swallow,
and laments the necessity of skipping
at least two courses if he wishes to
make a few remarks to the lady whom
he escorted to the table.

There is a medium between these
two extremes, which should be the
aim of the hostess to achieve. The
three-hours' dinner is now, or should
be, practically a thing of the past, and
this without any excessive acceleration
of the service. Soup, fish, *entrée*, joint,
game, sweet, savoury, suffice to any
man, and even the public diner must
sometimes feel that time lags heavily
throughout the immoderate length of
the company or civic banquet. I have
noticed that at one or two
dinners of late either fish
or soup has been omitted.
This struck me as a pecu-

Fish or soup
sometimes
dispensed
with.

liarly sensible plan, because it is these
two initial courses that absorb so much
time. Such reforms as these are not
readily adopted by the world in
general ; but, when one comes to think
of it, soup is really unnecessary, and
even out of place, on a hot summer

evening, and fish is not such a universal favourite as to be very generally missed from the menu of an excellent dinner.

Hors d'œuvres of the pickled

Hors d'œuvres now often omitted. variety are condemned by many as an extremely bad introduction to a varied meal, and now that oysters are fallen into disrepute the *hors d'œuvre* is often conspicuous by its absence. This economises at least from five to ten minutes at the beginning of the dinner; but, on the other hand, the temperature of the soup often suffers from the absence of the " whets," which allow the cook to keep it hot until the last moment. If we look at one of the menus of fifteen years since, the difference between this and the ones to which we are now accustomed will be apparent enough. The large number of side dishes and the necessarily varied choice of vegetables are characteristics which have now, fortunately, disappeared. No one ever heard in those days, or at least very rarely, of the vegetable *entrée* which now so often replaces those of fish or meat, and another point in favour of our own time is the interesting

Salads entail no delay. variety of salads which now appear, these being no hindrance to the rapidity of the dinner, since they are handed round with the cheese course.

Menu-builders should remember that white soups into which milk or cream enters as a component part should never follow *hors d'œuvres* of which fish forms an ingredient, such as caviare, oysters, lax, or the Norwegian herrings. In fact, there are various indictments against any sort of thick soup. Nearly all true gastronomes prefer a *consommé* to a thick preparation for the commencement of the principal meal of the day. It is only the aldermanic digestion which can satisfactorily cope with a thick soup. However, there is usually a choice, a clear soup being generally available.

"There are various indictments against thick soups."

Turbot is at present the most popular all-year-round dinner fish for ceremonious occasions. Salmon should be given precedence, but it is usually so extremely expensive as to be far beyond the price of all but the very wealthy, who need no hints on dinner giving. Turbot used at one time to be invariably served with lobster sauce, a preparation which was very much too solid, and, besides, to a certain extent, injured the distinctive flavour of the turbot. It is now more usual to send it to table with a sauce made of dissolved butter, in which a little anchovy or yolk of egg has been deftly mingled. Whitebait taxes to some extent the skill of the ordinary cook in frying, yet it is worth some trouble, as it is such a general

Lobster sauce with turbot not general now.

95

favourite. If only one fish is served it
is sometimes followed by a fish *entrée*
or cream ; and here a little
Fish cream. word of warning may be
given to hostesses to beware of offering
too many of these light preparations to
their guests. The mode of preparing
these creams, namely, by pounding the
fish in a mortar and rendering it so
readily digestible, is not always favour-
able to the welfare of the eater. Dentists
tell us our teeth would be in much
better order if we gave them tougher
work to do. These creams give them
nothing whatever to do, and the very
tender and succulent meats which it is
the aim of the good cook to send to
table also tend to place our teeth in the
position of Othello, whose occupation
was gone.

At some houses the *entrée* precedes
the joint, while at others it follows it.
There will always be a
**Joints now
often replaced** difference of opinion on
by lighter this matter among hostesses,
dishes. and it is a question which
every one can be left to settle for
herself. What is more to the pur-
pose is the fact that a joint is now
often replaced by a dish of much
lighter character — pheasants, wood-
cock, grouse, or partridge, when in
season, guinea fowl, &c. This is an
innovation of which physiologists ap-
prove. Most of us eat too much meat,
and the later the dinner-hour the more
injurious is this quantity. It will be

found that dinner as a meal is gradually assimilating the characteristics of supper, as in the banishment of the heavier forms of food, the curtailment of the sweet course and the disappearance of dessert. It is to be regretted that the fruit does not appear to a greater extent upon the luncheon table now that it is so slightly represented at the dinner-table. It is too valuable, dietetically considered, to be with impunity omitted from the programme of our daily fare. In America it appears at breakfast, an example we should do well to follow with the fruits that are legitimately in season in our own land.

Fruit used for breakfast in America.

The savoury now attracts more attention than dessert, and the hostess who can present a new one to her guests achieves a momentary renown. This is one of the many changes that have passed over the dinner table of late.

OUR modern modes of exercising hospitality would be a revelation indeed to our ancestors of forty, or even thirty years since. They lived in large houses, when the exchequer permitted, and kept up a staff of servants, in order that they might entertain their friends and acquaintances in their home. The size of the dining-room, and the question of how many it would seat at dinner, was a highly important one ; and the amount of rent paid for accommodation, far extra to the daily needs, was enormous. Not only financially, but in other matters, did this state of things tend to the elaboration of existence. The lady of the house found her mornings absorbed in the care of a huge mansion, with a sufficient staff of servants to keep it in order, and had on her hands, besides, the care of whole regiments of glass and china, adequate to the hospitality entailed by her position. The best dinner service and the every-day one, the cut-glass decanters, tumblers, and wineglasses, the silver and the plate, had to be kept in condition, even though dinner parties

Entertaining, forty years ago.

Elaborate machinery.

or ball suppers occurred no oftener than half a dozen times in a twelvemonth. But there is now a great and agreeable simplification of the machinery of hospitality. Partly due, probably, to the restricted space of the ordinary fashionable flat, this has developed into a means of relief from a heavy burden. Empty houses are utilised for dances, and the domestic upheaval of giving them in one's own home is thus avoided. Sets of rooms are arranged at all the large hotels, where private people may hold dances, give dinners, wedding breakfasts, or wedding teas. Less ambitious, but equally convenient for the owners of limited incomes, are the smaller rooms to be found all over London and the larger cities, and available at rates proportionate with their size and situation. It is no longer necessary to keep up a large establishment and live in a huge house in order to show hospitality. The dining-table that "seats twenty" is not much in demand, save among the most exclusive, conservative, and aristocratic grades of society. The old rule that dinner parties should consist numerically of never less than the Graces, and never more than the Muses, is again in force, and when a "big" dinner has to be given, the only trouble involved to

Modern entertainments much simpler for the hostess.

Dances, &c., are "contracted out."

"Never less than the Graces, never more than the Muses."

host and hostess is that of making out
the list of guests, fixing on the evening,
deciding on the rooms where it shall
be given, and settling details with the
manager of the hotel, or in the case of
suites apart from hotels, arranging with
the caterers as to the price to be paid
per head, and the items of the menu.
The development of the caterers' trade
has been enormous during the last
fifteen years, and the large
amount of competition has
brought down prices from
the immoderate figure at
which they stood even in the seventies.
And not only are charges lowered, but
every detail of the entertainment is
taken off the hands of the host and
hostess, whether it be the case of a
coming of age entertainment to hundreds of persons, or a small dinner of
nine or ten people in the home.
Napery, glass, china, flowers, plates,
dishes, ornaments, artistic lights, the
shades in harmony with the
furnishings and draperies of
the room, wines, waters,
seats, and attendance, are
all included in the list of things that
can be supplied. Even the menu cards
and stands can be arranged for, and in
some cases the invitations are sent out
from a list handed over by the host or
hostess. The relief thus extended to
the hospitable, or those obliged by the
necessities of a conventional society to
entertain merely as a *quid pro quo*,

Importance of the catering trade.

Caterers will, if required, furnish everything.

without any inspiration of real hospitality, is very great. To be able to live in a small house, and keep two or three servants, instead of half a dozen women and a butler, to say nothing of a footman or two, involves in itself an immunity from expense and a freedom from housewifely cares that can scarcely be conceived of by those who have never dined and danced their friends under the old conditions. To have the house turned upside down for a ball is almost unknown now. In town a set of rooms is hired, except in the case of great people whose establishment **A modern country ball.** includes a ball-room. In the country a marquee is erected, the caterers undertaking everything, from the erection of the tent and its decoration, and lighting, and ventilation, down to the minutest detail, including the music, the programmes, and the hat-shelves for the guests. Very rarely indeed now does the hostess cover her supper table with dainties prepared in her own kitchen, as was the custom before all these new developments arose. Many a ball was preceded by two or three days' hard work in the kitchen, **The hard work formerly entailed,** superintending and occasionally taking an active part in the preparation of pasties, tarts, jellies, creams, méringues, blanc-manges, and providing the salads, even to the home-made dressing, the hams, fowls, galantines, game, and so on, as may be gathered from any cookery book of the time. When the ball opened, the lady of the house was often almost prostrated with fatigue; and instead of being at her brightest to entertain her friends, was more or less a wreck, owing to her exertions and the inevitable worry of providing eatables on such a large scale. The mere arrangement of the flowers was often an exhausting task for the hostess and her daughters. Professional **Now undertaken by professionals.** hands now do it all, with a speed that is the result of constant practice, and at charges that even the middle-class hostess finds preferable to the care and fatigue, to say nothing of the less artistic results, of undertaking it herself.

And again, much domestic stress is avoided by the growing habit of men's dinners being held at clubs **Club dinners.** or hotels, whether the party consist of a duet or run into numbers. The telegram " Bringing home two men to dinner," is now replaced by " Dine at club to-night ; don't expect me," involving not only an agreeable immunity from added cares, but a pleasant freedom to dispense entirely with dinner, and substitute a meal of tea and muffins in its place, **The new order of things.** with a favourite book tilted up against the teapot for convenient perusal. Who would exchange the new order of things for the "good old times"? The mere thinking out of the bill of fare was troublesome in those days, when the art of cookery had not been exhaustively studied as now it is. The caterers send in several lists to choose from, with price per head appended, and the only trouble is to select the menu from those submitted for choice.

In the old days, hampers for the Derby or for picnic excursions were packed **Even for the** with comestibles prepared at **Derby or** home. Sometimes the task **picnics** of providing the food was shared among the organisers of the affair, with the consequence that something was almost always forgotten. But now the caterer steps in with his admirable organisation, and the affair is complete. Even the boiling water **The ubiqui-** that now appears at every **tous caterer** meal for the dyspeptic's in-**steps in.** dispensable beverage is at hand when called for. The table rises like magic from under the lid of the picnic hamper. The butter emerges from a cool retreat, glass-lined, within its own particular box. The salt, without whose savour many a dead and gone picnic had to be content, is provided in sufficiency in receptacles with tightly-fitting lids. The whole paraphernalia for tea in the woods or on the river is supplied in the same way, No longer is it necessary to make a fire of dry sticks and boil the water over it. Safety spirit-lamps with draught-proof stands take the place of

the old primitive fashion, and if something of improvisation and
The stick-and- extemporaneous be missing
tripod fire
replaced by the from the picnic of to-day,
spirit-lamp they are qualities appreciated only by the very young. The
certainty of tea is preferred by the
majority. In these and many other
ways the simplification of hospitality
progresses, and in view of the pace at
which life rushes along at this end of
the century, it must be well that simpler
modes should replace the troublesome
elaborations of a couple of decades
since. Supper at a hotel restaurant is now
accepted as the equivalent of a dinner
invitation. The frequent instances of
the sale of large town houses belonging
to wealthy noblemen may possibly be
intimately connected with
And the hotel this revolution in modes of
restaurant
supper takes entertaining. They can en-
the place of a tertain their personal friends
house dinner.
in sumptuously decorated
and brightly illuminated hotel restaurants, with fountains, flowers, and
palms for supplementary adornments.
and for banquets they have choice of
splendid rooms in large hotels. With
these the necessity for keeping up a
large town house is removed, and, glad
to be free of its charges, they sell it to
some millionaire, and, for their own
part, are content to put up at some
luxurious central hotel on their visits to
town.

AT HOMES.

WHEN first invitations were sent out on folded notepaper or in an ungummed envelope, permitting the expense of the postage to be defrayed by a half-penny stamp, everybody cried, "How mean!" But it is no longer considered so. In fact, there is a sort of snobbishness in the frame of mind that ex-

Economy no longer considered mean.

presses itself in disapproval of anything that savours of economy. There are persons who would not for worlds be seen sitting on one of the benches in Hyde Park, however comfortable it might be, lest any one should suspect them of unwillingness or inability to pay a penny for a chair. And there are people so afraid of being considered economical that, if writing at the same time to three or four members of the same family, they invariably

The really snobbish act.

put the letters in three or four envelopes, with a separate stamp on each. But this kind of thing is really snobbish. It is only into matters of hospitality that economy must never enter.

The modern invitation may, therefore, be sent out under cover for a half-penny stamp, since this in no way affects the convenience of the recipient. The usual form is a card measuring five inches by four. Printed in-

Form of invitation card. vitation cards, as used in the best society, are in copper-plate, and read as follows :—

MRS. CAUDLEY-BROWN

AT HOME

Thursday, June 29th.

4 TILL 7.

200, Ridley Square.

R.S.V.P.

The names of the invited persons are written at the top, above those of the

Guest's name. hostess. If the At Home is to be held at any other place than the residence of the hostess, the words explaining this appear under the

Place of entertainment. line giving date and hour— "at the Grafton Galleries," for instance, and in this case it is usual to put : "R.S.V.P. to 300, Ridley Square," or whatever the address may be.

If any special entertainment is provided for the guests, they are apprised of it by a line in the lower right-hand

corner. "Music," "Comédie Française," or the name of some fashionable reciter, singer, violinist, dramatic artist, &c., may occupy this position. If the performer be of very high distinction in his or her profession, the cards are sometimes worded—

Special entertainment.

"To meet Signor Sonofacio,"
or "To meet Madame Delizia."

In the case of royalty or guests of very high rank this line is phrased—

To meet royalty.

"To have the honour of meeting
Their Royal Highnesses the Duke
and Duchess of Quelquechose."

Should the announcement be dancing, the hour when it is to begin is stated on the invitation, and is very often followed by the hour when carriages are to be ordered. As this :

Dancing.

"Dancing 9.30.

Carriages 4 o'clock."

I append here menus for an Ascot party, a luncheon at Lord's, a launch party, and a boating party. The refreshments at an ordinary afternoon "At Home" are similar to those already dealt with under the heading of "Wedding Receptions."

Refreshments.

AN ASCOT PARTY.

———

Salade de Homard.
Saumon, Sauce Raifort glacé.
Bœuf rôti.
Pâté de Poularde et Pigeon.
Poulets rôtis.
Langues de Bœuf.
Asperges Marinés.
Côtelettes à la Connaught.

———

Sandwiches variés.

———

Méringues à la Crême.
Bouchées Pralinées.
Eclairs au chocolat.

———

Fraises et Crême.

———

GLACES.
Crême de Fraises.
Eau de Limon.

———

Limonade.

———

Thé et Café.

———

Gâteaux et Biscuits

LORD'S.

———

Saumon à la Zingari.
Salade de Homard.

———

Chaudfroids de Cailles à la Royale.
Poulets rôtis aux Cresson.
Galantines de Volaille.
Jambon de York.

———

SANDWICHES.
Aux Cresson.   de Langues.
Croûtes de Foies Gras.

AT HOMES.

Gelées aux Fruits.
Crêmes variées.

GLACES.
Crême de Fraises.
Eau de Muscat.
Café Glacé.

Limonade.

Thé (chaud).
Gâteaux et Biscuits.

BOATING PARTY

LUNCHEON AT 1.

Mayonnaise de Homard.
Saumon, Sauce Tartare.
Cailles farcis aux Truffes.
Poulets rôtis.
Langues de Bœuf.
Targe d'Agneau.
Fraises et Crême.

TEA AT 4.
Strawberry Cream Ice.
Lemon Water Ice.
Iced Coffee.
Tea.
Bread and Butter.
Cakes and Biscuits.

SUPPER AT 8.
Poulets à la Béchamel.
Bœuf épicé.
Salades Françaises.
Gelées aux Fruits.
Petits Fours.
Fraises et Crême.

LAUNCH PARTY.

———

	Bonne Bouche de Crevettes.
Xeres Sec.	Mousse de Foies gras.
	Tomâtes Marinades.

———

	Saumon, Sauce Verte.
	Homard à la Patti.
	Salade.

Haut Sauterne.

———

	Cailles en Caisses.
	Poulets rôtis aux Cresson.
	Langue de Bœuf.

———

Pommery and Greno, 1889.	Ponche à la Romaine.

———

	Targe d'Agneau.
	Pois à la Marinés.
	Sirloin de Bœuf.

———

Magnums Bollinger, 1884.	Pâtisseries Genoises.

———

Benedictine, Crême de Cacao.	Glaces Variées.

———

Liqueur Brandy, 1875.	Café Froid.

———

Clos de Vougeot, 1888.	Gâteaux Variés.
Château Lafite, 1877.	Biscuits Assortis.
	Bread and Butter.

———

Gallinari.	Fruits.
Port (Crofts), 1863.	

———

Thé et Café (chaud.)

At balls there is always a refreshment buffet, as well as a regular supper.

Refreshments at balls. Generally everything is cold at supper, but sometimes in winter hot soup is provided in cups, more particularly when the giver of the ball lives in the country, and a long drive lies before most of the guests.

A merciful custom has been adopted of late years when balls are kept up till 3 or 4 a.m. The hostess arranges with the keeper of a coffee-stall for refreshments of a simple but comfortable kind to be supplied to the coachmen and footmen of her guests, whose long, weary wait outside is thus beguiled of at least one of its disagreeables, hunger. May it be suggested that the horses should be released from the galling curb at such times, even if in the daytime the vanity of their owners imposes these cruel things upon the unfortunate animals.

CHILDREN'S PARTIES.

CHILDREN's parties are now almost always held at a sensible hour, permitting the little ones to be home and in bed by nine o'clock. From four till seven or eight is the usual time. They have tea, or chocolate, or milk at a buffet when they arrive, and at seven o'clock they all sit down to supper. This is ever so much better than the old style, under which juvenile parties were held in the evening, finishing at 10 p.m. The fare, too, has improved in character, without being less inviting. There is hardly any pastry to be seen on the youngsters' supper table. Its place is filled by cakes of all kinds, chocolate, fruit, cherry, almond, and sponge cake, treated with splendid decorativeness in sugar, pink and white with hollowed centre filled with whipped cream, sliced banana and pine, crystallised cherries, and chopped pistachio. These may not be the most digestible things in the world, but they are at least better than the old-fashioned pastry, thick and heavy, one of the greatest enemies of the human digestion ever invented.

Early hours prevail.

Improvements in the fare.

Creams and jellies should always occupy prominent positions on the table at children's parties. They attract by their prettiness, and, if well made, should be both nourishing and digestible. Jellies especially appeal to the childish imagination by their transparent delicacy of aspect, and it is almost cruel to provide insufficient to go all round. I have seen such longing eyes fixed on the swiftly diminishing, quivering mound as it is handed round, and have known perfectly well that this longing came, not from greediness, but from an innate love of beauty. Hostesses of the Lilliputs! Do have plenty of jelly, amber-clear and rosy-red, sparkling like jewels, and saying many beautiful things to the minds of children that you and I once used to hear, but have long ago forgotten.

Jellies should be plentiful.

There was a time when children at parties disdained such commonplace food as plain bread-and-butter, but for some reason which it is impossible to fathom, it is always now in great demand. Little boys, in particular, look around for it amid the varied supply of good and pretty things, and usually both begin and finish with a substantial layer of this every-day preparation. "Bread-and-butter, please," is their response to all invitations to discuss cake. Even the exciting joys of crackers are post-

"Bread and butter, please."

poned until due attention has been paid to the plain fare. A hint of the fact to hostesses is enough.

Another very favourite form of food is to be found in mixed biscuits, the sort

Mixed biscuits. that has sugared ornaments lavished on them in varied colours and designs. Pink sugar is always the first to disappear. Children adore pink both in dress and food. Pink méringues are almost always selected in preference to the white or coffee-coloured. Birthday cakes should always have pink icing on the top, with the name of the birthday boy or girl spelt out in preserved cherries. A row of edible pearls round the edge is regarded as a very great embellishment in the eyes of the Lilliputs. The "pearls" are sugar merely, but they look quite lovely and taste very well.

The beautiful open-mindedness and sincerity of childhood are refreshing enough. Some elders laughed heartily

The sincerity of childhood. over an instance of this at a fancy ball, where one of the stewards, having asked a group of little girls if they would like him to get them partners, was eagerly followed all round the room by them, some of them running to keep up with him, as he hunted out boys for them. A few years hence they will all have learned to dissimulate this very natural anxiety to enjoy a dance. And while we laughed, we also sighed to think that social exigencies should necessitate any such clouding over of the beautiful, transparent truthfulness that makes the company of a child such a delightful rest to many of us. It has not yet learned that "speech was given to us to conceal our thoughts," and in its talk we sometimes get a glimpse of the beautiful world in which children live —a land where our great things are small, our small things great, and the atmosphere is radiant with "the light that never shone on land or sea."

" Are there giants in the valley—
 Vale of childhood, where you dwell ?
Is it calm in that green valley,
 Round whose bourne such great hills swell ?

Are there giants in the valley—
 Giants leaving footprints yet ?
Are there angels in the valley ?
 O, tell me ! I forget."

AT A RESTAURANT.

THE development of restaurant life in London proceeds apace. To dine out three or four nights a week

Practice of dining at restaurants becoming more general.

at some of the palatial establishments is not unusual, and that, too, in a grade of society that was once of the most domestic order. Perhaps the general unsatisfactoriness of cooks has something to do with it. It used to drive a man to his club. The only difference is that now it drives him and his wife to a restaurant, where they are certain to find a good dinner. And is it eventually a more costly business than keeping a high-waged cook

Not perhaps more costly than a high-waged cook.

whose perquisites alone are a heavy item, and who insists on having underlings to do all but the highly-scientific parts of her work for her? It is far better to have a cook who can manage a few dishes with skill and finish, and who is independent of kitchenmaids and all their works, their innumerable breakages, their wastefulness, and their destructiveness.

A little dinner at a smart restaurant

116

is a pleasant break in the monotony of the weekly home pro-

A pleasant break for husband and wife. gramme. It affords topics of conversation to husband and wife, apart from business and domestic worries ; and the mere change of food is often a factor in promoting health and digestion. Home housekeeping is apt to become very groovey, and the same dishes reappear with constant iteration on the same oak or mahogany table. Many a new idea for the preparation of food is picked up at a good restaurant, with great advantage to the home dinners.

The new plan of giving a wine course, adopted at at least one cf the great London restaurants,

A wine course. is so excellent that one wonders why it has never been done before. As at a dinner-party, there is sherry with the soup, followed by a choice between hock and claret, a couple of glasses of champagne, and a liqueur. With a fixed price for this wine course, varying according to quality, but distinctly stated on the card, one knows exactly where one is.

It is often a very convenient plan to entertain friends at a restaurant instead of at one's own home, especially when

The guest moves first at a restaurant party. hostess and guest live at extreme ends of London. The guest must remember that on such occasions it is her duty to make the move after the meal, instead of its devolving upon the hostess. The reason of this is that the move from the table breaks up the party and the hostess cannot, for that reason, make it. The principal guest of the ladies present must do so.

The exception to this rule is when the party has been arranged for "dinner and play." In this case the hostess makes the move at the conclusion of the meal.

It is scarcely necessary to add that very loud talking and laughing, and all personal remarks about absent acquaintances, are in the very worst of taste at a restaurant. It is a matter in which well-bred people are not at all likely to err.

AT THE CLUB.

WOMEN'S clubs are among the new developments of the late Victorian Era,

Women's clubs. which has done such wonders for women. The first feeling of disapproval with which they were regarded, an inevitable attitude towards anything that is new, has now given place to an acknowledged conviction of their undoubted utility. Even those who regard them as pernicious institutions so far as married women are concerned are fain to confess that club life has marvellously brightened the lonely lives of the unmarried and widows of the leisured classes. The etiquette of club life presents few difficulties. Any one wishing to be elected has only to send to the secretary of the special club to

Election. which she wishes to belong for the necessary form to fill up, and to find a friend who is already a member to propose her, and another friend to second her. It would constitute a serious breach of etiquette to send in the name of any friend or acquaintance as referee without previously obtaining her permission to do so. It may be considered unnecessary

to mention this, but the records of
more than one club prove that such
an occurrence is not un-
known. A copy of the rules
should be procured and studied before
visiting the club, and good manners
oblige one to carefully abide by them.
More heart - burning and dissension
has arisen among members from this
cause than from any other. It should
be borne in mind that gratuities are never given to
club servants, at least to those who
wait at table. Just at first, when the
member is new to club life, she is
apt to give at the close of a meal what
she has been accustomed to do when
lunching, having tea or dining at a
restaurant. But all precedent is against
the practice.

Club life offers almost as many
opportunities for the practice of unselfishness as home life.
Marriage itself is scarcely
better adapted for the cultivation of this excellent quality. There
are many temptations to selfishness
that may be overcome or yielded to
according to disposition. An accusation has been brought against club life
to the effect that it encourages selfishness, and this may possibly have some
foundation in fact, especially
with regard to men's clubs,
but the very fact that the
soil is a good one for the
growth of so noxious a weed proves

The rules.

Gratuities.

A school for
unselfishness.

Where
weeds flourish,
flowers will
bloom.

that the circumstances are such as will tell well in favour of the skilful gardener who cultivates only the best in the ground at his disposal. I have heard that it is particularly with regard to newspapers that men are prone to exhibit selfishness at their clubs, but women, as a rule, are not very fond of newspapers. There are various matters, however, in which a fine disregard of the rights of others may be displayed. I may, perhaps, be forgiven if I refer to one, viz., the looking-glass.

Monopolising the looking-glass. It is very aggravating, when one wants only the tiniest peep, just to see that all is neat and tidy, to be kept away for ever so long by some one who apparently needs half an hour's pulling together before she can consider herself fit to be seen. At Sandown I have often noticed this sort of selfishness, which is particularly irritating when a male escort is waiting outside with that impatience that, if not peculiar to race days, is apt to be more pronounced on such occasions. And

Male inconsistency. yet it is these very men who would be annoyed if a crooked bonnet or a wildly flying feather, an unhinged shoe-lace or refractory waistband, were to spoil the effect of a careful toilette. Men are most particular about the general "get-up" of the fortunate women who share their walks and rides, their rows and drives,

their outdoor and their indoor plea-
sures. With a pleasing inconsistency
they gibe at fashions of every sort,
whether sensible or the reverse, but
are excessively annoyed if their
womenkind do not faithfully follow
them.

Many pleasant acquaintances are
sometimes made at clubs. However,
it is argued by some that
Idleness and club life. women's clubs are only
covers for idleness, and
that they induce many to neglect the
duties of the home. But if a woman
is naturally inclined to be idle she
will be even more attracted by it at
home than at the club; and, after all,
active idleness—that which takes one
out into the world to see fresh sights,
hear fresh sounds, exchange ideas, and,
in fact, live rather than vegetate—is
ever so much to be preferred to passive
idleness. The numerous ladies' clubs
in London are the resort of some of
the busiest women to be
The resort of the busiest of women. found among our great city's
four million and a half in-
habitants. One or two, it is
true, are devoted to the wealthy and
the frivolous classes, but even among
these there is a good proportion of
members who make a business of
philanthropy; a development that,
though not peculiar to our Queen's
reign, has astonishingly increased during the last fifty years. A Royal
Princess belongs to one of these

clubs. She and her daughter had tea there not long since, after having had a drive of some miles to open a charitable institution.

One wonders what the Queen's own opinion is about clubs for women. Her Majesty would probably *The Queen's view of clubs.* incline to condemn them, knowing little of the domestic routine of the upper middle-classes, and still less about the lives of the educated women who support themselves by remunerative occupations such as lecturing, book reviewing, book producing, academic pursuits, journalism, dressmaking, and millinery. Such as these are often entirely dependent upon their club for companionship. And in all ranks there are to be found the widows, the spinsters, and what a French writer happily calls the "*mal-mariées*," whose leisure is much too abundant for enjoyment. They have few duties, and scarcely know how to dispose of the long hours of every day. What a boon a club is to such as these ; though, it must be admitted, these sometimes depressed individuals are not always a boon to the club.

CORRESPONDENCE.

In nothing are the qualities of a gentlewoman, as such, more apparent than her correspondence.

Correspondence reveals character. In forming our estimate of an unknown person from whom we receive a letter, we judge her, first by the character of her notepaper, the neatness or otherwise of the lettering composing the address, and even more than all, by the composition of the note itself. It needs some practice to say in a letter exactly what has to be said, with no more discursiveness than may be necessary to avoid an appearance of abruptness.

Tact. The bright and shining quality of tact is as useful here as in other matters. One often hears the phrase, "It is the letter of a lady," applied to some missive which may relate purely to business, and yet denote the cultivated qualities of the writer.

Orthography. A point in which one should be very particular is the correct spelling of the names of those whom one addresses. Many persons are extremely sensitive on this matter. And in another, though a minor matter, it is well to observe the Golden Rule which applies to every action of our lives ; and which is often abbreviated to—

" Do as you'd be done by."

I refer to the addresses on the envelopes we send off. They should be copied from those on our correspondent's own note-paper or visiting-cards with as much accuracy as the names themselves. Why should some of us grudge our acquaintances the small satisfaction of having their residence described as being in South Belgravia instead of Pimlico, in Kensington rather than in Notting Hill, and in the neighbourhood of Portland Place in preference to that of Great Portland Street ? It is the ambition of every one of us to make as good an appearance in all things appertaining to our social position as circumstances may permit. A good address is among the desirable circumstances of our surroundings, and there is no harm whatever in describing our locality in the best possible fashion. But to hear some of the disagreeable remarks occasionally made in such cases, one might imagine it to be a piece of what is popularly known as "side." "I'm not going to do anything so idiotic as to address her at

The golden rule applied to addressing.

To make a good appearance a general desire.

Something Street, Cavendish Square, when she really lives in a back street out of Marylebone High Street," is the sort of thing that ill-natured persons sometimes say. But ill-nature is always an enemy of good manners.

Ill-nature always opposed to good manners.

As I have said elsewhere, plain but good cream-coloured notepaper is always in the best taste, with no crest, and the address either thickly embossed in white or printed in one colour, the characters being as distinct as possible, but not immensely large or straggling. No crest should appear on it. Unmarried women and widows have practically no crest. A wife uses that of her husband if she uses any, but it is not usual for any one in really good society to allow it to appear on notepaper or invitation cards.

The note-paper.

Crests should not be used.

It used to be considered rather rude to conclude a letter on the first or second page. If our grandfathers or grandmothers did so, they almost invariably apologised for a brevity that in those days had the effect of curtness. Nowadays, however, we live at such high pressure that it is only from friends living abroad that we ever expect a real letter. Notes of half a dozen lines, or at most covering two sides of the paper, are the most

Brevity not bad form.

usual form of correspondence, and the blank half-sheet is at the disposal of the thrifty, who tear it off and put it away with dozens of others that, in the last generation, would have been scrupulously covered from a sense of politeness.

Notepaper prepared for hostesses of country houses has almost always in one corner the name of the nearest station and that of the nearest post town or telegraph station. But it is courteous, even when not residing in the country, to give the clearest possible directions to new acquaintances as to the best mode of reaching one's house, whether to make a morning call or to attend a dinner-party. It is really a flagrant omission to fail in this, when one lives on the outskirts of great, over-grown London, and it is well to particularise the best mode of conveyance, not omitting, if an afternoon call be in question, the humble omnibus. This vehicle used to be disdained by gentlewomen, but the wave of democracy that has of late swept over us has allowed us to perceive the utility of this among other cheap things. It may be a question if well-dressed women have really the right to occupy seats in these public vehicles to the frequent exclusion of the poorer sisters for whose convenience they were

Country-house notepaper.

Indicating conveyances.

The humble 'bus becoming fashionable.

intended. When one sees a working woman or a tired-looking *Its use may sometimes be unfair.* working man with his bag of tools turned away from an omnibus full of gaily-garbed' women, one cannot fail to suspect an injustice.

The post-card has been regarded as largely responsible for the curt brevity of modern correspondence ; but it is really the effect, rather than the cause, of the limited interchange of written words. The correspondence card and the letter-card are all consequences of the same rush and whirl in which we live. There is no time for letter-writing in these busy, scrambling days. The correspondence card is a boon indeed, but no gilt edges, if you please !

PRESENT-GIVING.

THERE is a gentle art in present-giving which is not always understood. Too **An art in present-giving not always understood.** many of us give rather what it suits us to bestow than what it suits the donee to receive. The poor relation is presented with some useless frippery in the shape of a dandified easel, be-ribboned and tinsel-draped, or a photograph frame mounted in pale brocade, for neither of which she has any real use, both being much too bright and fleeting in their brightness for daily use in "furnished apartments." Hampers are sent to the wealthy, instead of to those who really need the substantial contents, whether they consist of the seasonable poultry and ham or the equally appropriate wine and liqueurs, which would be so well appreciated by those whose daily fare seldom includes anything beyond the strictly necessary.

The fact is that purchasers of Christmas and birthday presents are prone to **The need of thought in the matter.** leave out the "thinking" part of the business, and to throw themselves heavily on chance for a choice. But there should go much thinking to every gift. It is the essence of present-making. "What would she like? What does he want? Has she ever expressed a particular wish for anything?" These are the questions that should be asked, instead of inconsequently hanging about shop counters and wondering "What can I give?" Very excellent suggestions may, it is true, be obtained in this way ; but these should be supplementary to the thinking, this last being a task to which indolent human nature is much averse.

The difficulty with some of our friends is that they have already presented themselves with everything they could possibly want or wish for, and nothing is left for others.

For the friends who have everything.

Such friends are bejewelled to such a degree as would render further acquisitions in that line surperfluous, if not worse, inviting them to an ostentatious display that savours of vulgarity. Their houses are replete with everything that money can buy. For them the only suitable gift is something out of the common, something that money alone cannot secure without the aid of travel in far lands and the opportunity it gives. There are shops in London where curios are to be found, the most precious of them stored away for certain appreciative customers, rare specimens of Eastern art, quaint pieces of old china, or metal work wrought

An old curio is best.

into strange, fantastic shapes. In old curiosity shops many a puzzled present seeker may find just what she wants— an antique, jewelled casket or châtelaine, vases so out of the common that they have a peculiar value as being almost unique, and strangely fashioned brackets in carton pierre, for which there is always room in even the most crowded of modern houses. Bits of jewellery in old paste, now growing so rare, are also to be picked up in these interesting shops, to say nothing of the long old-fashioned watch chains that are now in fashion again.

Then there are the poor, dear friends who want almost everything. One longs to bestow upon them a few luxuries, remembering the delightful saying of one in like case, "Give me the superfluities of life. I can then do without its necessaries." But the fallacy of this idea soon becomes but too apparent. I remember a case of a poor family which, in the depths of its poverty, retained that love of the beautiful which, in such circumstances, is a very doubtful blessing. An old friend kept them supplied, as well as she could, with food, often going dinnerless herself in order that they might at least have one good meal a day. Another friend of theirs brought them lovely baskets of flowers, costly things, received with acclamations of delight, caressed, and tended with

For the friends who have nothing.

peculiar care—grapes at three shillings a pound, or a basket of huge pears looking most decorative and appetising in their pale pink paper wrappings. This was part of "*le superflu, chose si nécessaire*," and the donor of the substantial meals used occasionally to wish that she, too, could give such graceful and poetic presents as these. But she went on in her usual course, doing what she could in the commissariat department, and did not know, till years afterwards, that the fruit and flowers cost the donor literally nothing. She became bankrupt, part of her liabilities being a large amount due to a fruiterer and florist. Hers was a good example of "how not to do it." She laid the recipients under a heavy obligation to herself, to which she had no real title.

Choose the necessaries of life.

With friends who are in real need money is not always the best gift. Good money's worth is often better. Nor is there any necessity to drive off sending it until the last moment, when Christmas is almost upon us, and when the poor souls have already made what tiny provision they could. Let the fine sirloin, the fat capon, the Yorkshire ham, the Cambridge sausages, the wine and whisky arrive by December 20th at least. Nothing will be allowed to spoil, of that we may be very sure. There will be immediate need of it

Money's worth often better than money.

and the Christmas fare will taste none
the worse if some of it should slightly
anticipate the actual day of the great
festival.

Men are very troublesome about
presents. One is often at a loss about
what to give them, especially
Presents for men. if they do not smoke. If
they do, there are all sorts
of openings for possible gifts, from
elaborately-fitted and highly expensive
smoking tables, and cigar boxes of
precious metals, down to such smaller
articles as cigar or cigarette cases, with
jewelled monogram on the leather
cover, and little match boxes. For the
people who like to do themselves
credit by giving showy presents there
are always lovely things to be found
at the stationers' shops—dressing-bags,
pocket-books, inkstands in gold and
crystal, ormolu and silver. But for
those who like to give useful, if unob-
trusive, things there remain such trifles
as a box of ties in favourite colours, a
dozen of the best and finest handker-
chiefs, embroidered with the initial
or monogram, half a dozen pair
of gloves in suède or kid, or even
A homely gift. a box of luxuriously warm,
soft socks, of such woolly
fineness, yet fibrous strength as to
afford the maximum of comfort with
longevity of wear, and a long-drawn
immunity from darns—a humble gift,
but one that at least has the
merit of proving consideration for the

recipient. There is nothing gaudy about it, is there? It is all very well for those who can afford it to walk into a jeweller's shop and choose a pretty diamond pin for husband or brother, but for one such there are a thousand others whose gifts have to be measured as the tailor cuts his coat—"according to his cloth."

Do not, then, let us shirk the preliminary thinking that goes far towards making a gift valuable, not only in suitability, but in carrying with it some of the very heart and mind of the giver. Why should we not rather give what is really needed or desired than what looks well, or seems to cost more than the true price? To choose for these reasons is really to make a present to ourselves of the appreciation of outsiders. But the inner heart of giving knows no such thought. It desires, above all, the good of the one who receives, ardently wishes to give pleasure, and forgets self completely in the delightful occupation of endeavouring to supply some long-felt want, or vague, half-formed wish on the part of those who cannot, or will not, spend money on themselves.

COUNTRY-HOUSE LIFE.

An invitation to a country house suggests all sorts of doubts to the inexperienced who have never before enjoyed this phase of English hospitality. The invitations are almost always explicit about the term of the visit,

Accepting these invitations. and the reply should be so worded as to convey to the hostess the visitor's acceptance of the same, including the date of its termination. The dresses taken must be in accordance with the

The dresses taken. social status of the hostess, and it is indispensable that every garment should be fresh and neat, even if it be not costly. No hostess is so unreasonable as to expect elaborate toilettes to be worn by those of her guests whom she knows to be ill-endowed with this world's gear.

In the hall of the usual country house there is a card, often of the fashionable poster order, and more or less ornamentally framed,

Postal and train service card. on which the hours of postal deliveries and collections are clearly printed. Sometimes the train service from and to London and

other large towns in the vicinity are
given as well.

THE HOSTESS.

FROM THE GUEST'S POINT OF VIEW.

Modern manners are so free and easy
that the country-house hostess is often
almost ignored by her fashionable
guests. Unless she chances to be a
woman possessing some force of character, her good nature is taken advantage of, and she is induced to send out
invitations to friends of her guests,
unknown to herself, and the results are
sometimes far from pleasant. The fast
and furious fun that goes on at some of
these country-house parties may be in
the highest degree disagreeable to her,
but, having given the invitations to the
persons who originate and enjoy the
practical joke form of pastime, she is
helpless and powerless during the re-
mainder of their stay. The ideal hostess
has always sufficient force
of character to steer clear
of such difficulties, but, truth
to tell, there are some
country-house châtelaines who thoroughly enjoy this kind of thing, and
who gather kindred spirits round them.
When a quiet-minded girl or young
married woman finds herself a member
of a party in which "ripping jokes"
and "screaming fun" are the order of
the day, and of half the night as well,
she is apt to be voted slow, and she
will certainly be thankful when her

*The ideal
hostess has
force
of character.*

visit comes to an end. But can anything be pleasanter than a stay at a really charming country house, where both host and hostess are well-mannered and well-bred, and where there is plenty of fun and amusement without any of the coarser element that vulgarises so many of the "stately homes of England"? Our upper middle classes—those to which the great bulk of military and naval officers belong, physicians, barristers, clergymen, and men who enjoy independent fortunes sufficient to enable them to enjoy lives of comparative luxury and leisure—are much cleaner and wholesomer in their lives and manners than the great mass of the high aristocracy. It is in the houses of the upper middle classes that true refinement is found, combined with luxurious appointments, and that exquisite, dainty cleanliness which, again, is much oftener found in this class than in what the French call "le hig life."

But one of the faults of the average hostess is fussiness. She often fails to realise that the happiness **Fussiness one of the faults of the average hostess.** of her guests is often in inverse ratio to the efforts made to secure it. To be allowed to go one's own way has always been a desire of human nature, and during a visit to the country there is sometimes a quite wearisome procession of drives and rides, tennis parties, garden parties, dinner parties, and boating parties, of which the guest gets heartily sick. Suppose that a London girl goes to stay at a country house after the fatigues of the season. Can anything be more delightful for her, or better adapted to her physical needs, than long, restful mornings, in which she can recuperate her energies and recover from the lassitude into which over-exertion in the cause of pleasure has thrown her? A choice of various forms of exercise may be offered to all in the afternoon, or, if repose is preferred at that time, then the riding, driving, boating, &c., be undertaken in the morning. Very often this fussiness arises from pure good-will and kindliness on the part of the châtelaine, but it is none the less a mistake.

"LETTERS TO WRITE."

One of the little social fictions which only the very harsh would call a real fib is often found in the above phrase when an excuse for escaping from some proposed expedition is sorely needed. The conscientious woman, after having declared that she must stay at home as she has letters to write, is not happy until she has written one or two, so that *The excuse convenient.* she may apply a saving salve to her conscience. And then come an hour or two of delicious rest, with the delightful sights and sounds of the country all about her, and that sense of leisure that seems unattainable in towns. The very frequency of the postman's knock is inimical to it, the official rat-tat at once suggesting thoughts of the letters to be answered, invitations to be accepted, and a host of other matters invading our calm. In the country house there are usually but two, or at most three, postal deliveries daily, and the "rat-tat" is seldom, if ever, heard. In the dulness of winter, country residents must often long for more posts, but when town folk go to rural districts for repose, one of the factors in their enjoyment is the rarity of them.

COUNTRY-HOUSE GUESTS.

FROM THE HOSTESS'S POINT OF VIEW.

A discontented face is a disagreeable sight anywhere, but more than ever so on board ship and in the country house. And some women, with everything life can give them—youth, health, riches, friends—make a habit of discontent, and spend half their time in grumbling. They seem to regard a wet day as a personal insult on the part of Providence. "So sure as I particularly wish it to be fine, it is certain to be wet," such a woman is often heard to say, and she is pretty sure to add, "Just my luck!" Wise hostesses carefully avoid all women who are given to such expressions as these, for they imply

The grumbler.

a discontented disposition. Another horror is the rude woman, who flatly contradicts every one who disagrees with her, makes unpleasant remarks, such as, "Dear me! You *have* changed since I saw you last!" or "That new hat does not suit you in the least;" or "How is it that your gowns never become you?" And next to her comes the censorious woman, who condemns everybody for everything they do. Nothing is ever right except what she does herself. On young people she is especially hard. If a girl accepts a man she is "extremely silly." If she refuses him she is "a perfect fool. Does the girl expect a duke?" If a young man makes a fresh start in life he is, according to these self-elected censors, "a rolling stone," and if he goes on in his groove he "has no energy, and will never do much in the world." Another of the hard bits for a hostess is when a mischief-maker is among her guests. She is worse than any of the rest, for she is usually so sly and such a story-teller that it is some time before she is found out, and not till considerable damage has been done. The bright, lively, good-natured and sympathetic girl or woman is always a welcome guest. The others are sure to be "dropped" after a while by hostess after hostess.

The question of tips to servants is

a vexed one. A young girl is not expected to give so much as a married woman. The amounts vary according to the social position of the hostess, rather than of the guest, in ordinary circumstances. In country houses belonging to persons of wealth the half-sovereign will be found a useful coin after a visit of a fortnight or so, but in case of a week-end visit a little silver is adequate to the occasion. Should the guest ride much the groom should not be forgotten ; and if her steed be an iron one the stable-boy who cleans it and polishes it is worthy of a dole. If the guest avail herself of the services of her hostess's lady's-maid, the latter will expect a gift. The coachman who drives her to the station will suggest by his manner, often a study in subtlety, that he is of opinion that his merits deserve financial notice. The butler who supervises the transport of one's luggage from upstairs to the hall cannot be overlooked any more than the housemaid who unstraps one's boxes and helps to lock them and strap them up. After a visit to town or country it is incumbent upon the guest to write within twenty-four hours of arrival elsewhere a note of warmly expressed thanks for the hospitality extended.

Tips to the servants.

The status of the hostess regulates the matter.

The horse attendants.

And house servants.

The vote of thanks on return.

TRAVELLING ABROAD.

ENGLAND is a great nation, as we all
know, but it is quite unnecessary for her
children, when they visit other countries, to put on airs of superiority, and
regard with contempt and disdain all
institutions that differ from our own.
'Arry's designation of all foreign tongues
is "their lingo," by which
Our
demeanour: phrase he probably intends
to express his conviction
that English ought to be spoken for
his convenience all over the world.
And Englishwomen wear too often an
expression of cold and critical dislike
when they allow their glance to fall
upon the women of other countries.
This is bad manners, wherever it may be
practised ; if in our own land, it becomes
an inhospitality ; if in other lands, it is
insulting rudeness. How badly our
countrywomen sometimes behave in
foreign churches is, unfortunately, but
too well known to those who go much
abroad. I have seen a poor old peasant
woman, disturbed at her devotions,
look up with a gaze full of wonder at
the loud chatter, and even laughter,
that are so unseemly in a place of
worship. And in a railway carriage a

bright, young German girl, stepping into a compartment in which a party of English were travelling, looked from one to the other with visible and increasing discomfort at their cold, unfriendly expression. We may feel absolutely convinced of our superiority to every other nation under the sun, but it is, to say the least, impolitic to allow our demeanour to convey the idea of that conviction to the inhabitants of the countries in which we find ourselves. A cosmopolitan friendliness, which never degenerates into familiarity, is a characteristic of the accustomed traveller, and it is usually the novice who thinks fit to arm herself with airs of supercilious superiority, hoping, perhaps, that strangers may accept her at her own valuation.

As to new acquaintances, considerable care should be exercised before **New acquaintances.** admitting them to anything resembling friendship or confidence; but this need not hinder the manner from being pleasant and the tone genial. Very agreeable acquaintances are sometimes made abroad, and should there be any indications of such, it is always well to give some information about oneself for the enlightenment of strangers. It can be indirectly offered, for this is one of the things that call for the exercise of tact.

The inexperienced traveller often falls a prey to bores, a race of beings who are to be found everywhere, and **The bores.** whose shadows never grow less. With practice, one learns to elude them without rudeness, even at table d'hôte. To be bored in a foreign language is a sad fate, to avoid which is well worth some study.

It ought to be a part of our patriotic feeling to endeavour to convey as agreeable an idea as possible of ourselves to those countries which we honour with our distinguished presence in our little trips. And we should find it to our advantage too. For the world reflects back upon us, as a rule, the sort of face we turn to it. If we scowl at large—and some of us really do— we shall find ourselves treated with scant courtesy.

Nothing is nicer than a neat tailor-made for travelling in. It should not **What to wear:** be of too thin or light a material, especially if there is a crossing of the Channel in question. There is always a cool breeze at sea, and the risk of chill is great. At table d'hôte a prettily made high bodice is worn, and a visit to the Casino is always made in a high-cut gown, never a *décolleté* one. Hats and toques are worn at the theatre, but sometimes the dresses in the private boxes are cut low, and at very smart seaside places the bodices are what dressmakers term " half-low."

ETIQUETTE OF MOURNING.

At first sight fashion would seem to have as little to do with mourning as it has with grief, but as those who wear the garb of woe are not invariably mourners in the strict sense of the term, fashion influences this form of dress very appreciably. Of late years the periods for wearing it have been very much abbreviated, and many other changes have taken place in what may be called for want of a better word the etiquette of mourning. It used, **An old rule now abolished.** for instance, to be a strictly observed rule that no member of the family who had just sustained a bereavement should put on deep mourning until a week after the death. The reason of this was that doing so would imply that the dresses had been prepared in advance in expectation of a death which might, after all, not have taken place. This would be a cold-blooded course of conduct which very few would be likely to adopt ; but now this old-fashioned prohibition is extinct. The making of mourning dresses is now conducted with such speed, as compared with the deliberate and leisurely mode of procedure of long ago, and money is so much more freely spent nowadays than it was in the thriftier times of our grandparents, that such a rule is naturally obsolete. The great houses that make a specialty of mourning costumes have every detail so well in hand that a few hours suffice to provide all that can be needed at the moment for the complete equipment of the mourners. Besides, black dresses are so very much worn in ordinary circumstances just now that there is generally some available compromise in the wardrobe. In the old days when the above-mentioned rule held good, very few people wore black gowns unless they were in mourning, or were widows well on in years. All

Texture of deep mourning dresses are in woollen materials, many of which are manufactured with a view to making them resemble the texture of crape as nearly as possible. The severity of outline that once characterised deep mourning dress is now replaced by a degree of elegance that would once have been considered inconsistent with the garb of grief.

Ultra smartness of the new mourning. An idea of ultra smartness is conveyed by new mourning, even that worn by widows in the first twelvemonth of their widowhood. Their dresses are made in the very height of the reigning fashion, and the widows' caps of to-day are but the light and

airy descendants of the uncompromis-
ingly large and heavily built ones of
thirty years ago. In those days a long
black shawl was indispensable in the
first days of deep mourning, and is
even now used during the first weeks
of bereavement by those who cling to
old customs ; but among the more
advanced in century-end ideas it is
replaced by smartly-cut capes or coats
heavily trimmed with crape. In fact,
so very fashionable and elegant is
modern mourning that the lavish use
of crape in its initial stages is an absolute necessity in order to distinguish it
from an ordinary black costume, such
as may be seen by the score in an
hour's turn in the Park on a summer

Headgear. morning. The headgear
remains distinctive, but far
less so than it used to be when bonnets
were crowded over with loops and
quillings of crape and sprays of flowers
made of the same material with occasionally a floral interlude, if so it may
be called, of black grapes composed
apparently of blow-glass in its most
fragile form.

It used to be an article of faith
that widows should wear black woollen

Gloves. gloves during the whole of
the first year after the husband's death ; but that was in the
days when *suède* gloves had not been
invented. The gloss of French kid
would have been considered incom-
patible with the dull blacks that custom

laid down as indispensable. Now,
suèdes and silk gloves are permitted,
and in a couple of months are suc-
ceeded by French kid. It is only
within the last twenty years that it has
been permitted to widows to lighten
the intensity of their weeds by the
addition of collar and cuffs

Collars and cuffs. of white batiste. Formerly
folds of black crape were
the only wear at the neck and wrists,
embroidered with jet after the first few
weeks, and not allowed to give place
to linen collars and cuffs until six
months had elapsed. It is now by no
means unusual to see widows wearing
linen collars a month after their bereavement. It is an age of unconven-
tionality in many ways, and when old
customs begin to be modified or re-
jected there are always those who take
advantage of transition periods and
commit flagrant errors in taste. Not
long ago a widow in deepest weeds
was present at a wed-

Mourning dress at weddings. ding, thus contravening all
the laws of good manners.
These rules may seem trivial
to many, but they are a crystallisation
in externals of kindheartedness and
those good manners that are "the fruit
of noble minds," and are worthy of
consideration. It is the bridegroom
who might feel aggrieved at the association of ideas caused by the presence
of a widow in weeds at his marriage.
There are thousands of men who can

view the prospect of death with serenity and calm, but there are few who on their wedding morning care to contemplate their bride in the character of a widow and themselves as inhabiting an early tomb.

In the periods of duration of mourning there have of late been radical changes. Widows' weeds used to be worn for a year and six months. It was then reduced to a year and a month, the vulgar reading of which was a year and a day. During the last few years deep crape and distinctive headgear have been dropped at the end of six months, the period known technically as "black silk" then setting in, this lasting for six months instead of three, as used to be the case when the very deep weeds were worn for a year. It is followed by three months of half-mourning, the changes in which are quite as radical as those of previous periods. In old days only grey, white, lavender, and a certain shade of violet were permissible, but now the introduction of mixed tints so numerous, and possessing such subtle affinities with each other has led to a state of things when practically almost any colour, save green, blue, and brown, may be worn with a black gown. Things seem tending towards the gradual elimination of what has always been called half-mourning, so closely has it approached of late to the character of the second period of Court

Duration of mourning.

mourning, regulated by the Queen, in which coloured ribbons, fans, flowers, and feathers are admissible with black dresses. Another change perceptible of late is in the type of dress **Dress worn by widows on re-marriage.** worn by widows on their re-marriage. In England white used to be forbidden to them, as it has been for time immemorial among the *bourgeoisie* of France, brides of higher rank in that country wearing on re-marriage a simply-made white dress with a long black lace veil falling over the face and covering the greater part of the back of the dress. An English widow of position, who recently re-married, wore white satin hemmed with sable, and a white velvet bonnet trimmed with the same fur.

There are those who advocate the abandonment of crape in deep mourning, pointing as an example **The use of crape.** to a Royal lady who refused to wear it when suffering bereavement some time ago. This is no valid argument so far as the general public are concerned. The use of crape is to announce to friends and acquaintances and others that our loss is so recent and our grief so acute that we must be excused from ordinary conversation or bearing our part as usual in the social or business world. It is the accepted sign of mourning, and its absence exposes the true mourner to inquiries and remarks that

probe the heart to its very depths. In
the case of the Royal lady in question,
every soul in the kingdom knew of her
loss and felt deepest sympathy with
her. Humbler mothers feel grief as
deep, though only a few of their immediate circle may be acquainted with
the circumstance, and for them the
wearing of crape is a necessary protection when they begin to go forth
into the world again after a short
period of necessary seclusion.

Here is another. It used to be a
canon of good manners that when an
acquaintance was perceived to be
wearing mourning no questions were
to be asked, no comment made, unless
the person whose recent loss was typi-
fied by black garments should broach
the subject. Very few ob-
serve this good old rule,
and yet it is one of the
principal reasons for putting on deep
black, and adding crape in cases of the
loss of a near relative.

A good old
rule.

Retirement from the world, even in
the first days of bereavement, is not
possible to us all, and the lightest
finger laid on one's burden of grief and
aching pain makes self-control most
difficult.

Even if the touch be sympathetic
and kindly—sometimes because it is so
—it is hard to bear, threatening to
break down the fortitude so hardly
won and only too easily lost.

It was Carlyle who wrote appreciatively of the "cheerful stoicism" of the cultivated classes of English society. But there are times that come to all of us, alas! when we can neither be cheerful nor stoical, try as hard as we may.

The correct periods for mourning, as observed in England by the upper middle classes are as fol-

The periods for mourning observed by upper middle class. lows :—For a husband : crape for a year, black for a year. For father or mother : crape for six months, black for three. For brother or sister : crape for three months, black for three. For son or daughter : crape for six or nine months, black for three more. For uncle, aunt, or niece : black for two months, modified black for one. For grandfather or grandmother : crape for three months, black for two. For cousin : black for two months.

These are the general rules for mourning, but it is needless to say that they are often modified by circumstances. Wives must remember that they wear mourning in the same degree for their husbands' relatives as for their own.

It is high time that some protest should be made against ladies attending the funerals of their husbands, fathers, brothers, or children. A man we know who was present at a recent sad occasion told

A protest. us that it was extremely painful to witness the terrible grief of the widow and her daughter, and that common humanity would have dictated their remaining at home as the proper course. Men have sometimes hard work to maintain their own fortitude, and it breaks them down to see the grief of the women mourners. In Ireland ladies seldom attend a funeral, and it seems to me that the ordeal is a much greater one than any girl or woman should suffer. Nor is there any reason that they should.

The feeling seems to be that staying away would infer a want of respect or affection to the dead. But if the custom were once established that the women of the family should not appear at funerals, it would be impossible to base any objection upon such a plea. Worn out with grief, and sometimes with fatigue after attendance upon a long illness of the lost one, there is no strength left to the mourner to resist her grief, and she breaks down pitifully just when she most desires to be calm and composed and to "possess her soul."

So long as the Queen sets the example, however, I suppose it is useless to protest. But it is just as well for those who disapprove to speak out and denounce the custom of dragging into publicity the grief that longs for solitude.

Is mourning going out of fashion? In what is called "smart" society the periods for wearing it are more

and more abbreviated, and the fabrics
and trimmings are much
Is mourning going out of fashion? less distinctive than they
used to be. We have all
been wearing black crêpon
for so long that things have become
rather mixed, and very often a costume
that looks like decided mourning is
simply black from choice, and is worn
with fawn gloves or a pink collar-band.
Even widows do not wear their weeds
nearly so long as was usual some years
ago, and they are seen in places of
amusement or in crowded "At Homes"
while still wearing deep mourning—
a thing that would not have been
tolerated by society ten years ago.

*   *   *

The whole matter is undergoing a
revolution—possibly some happy medium may be settled on by society ;
but, however it may be, the sensible
will take good care that mourning will
not become obsolete. It is too necessary, not only as a shield and protection
from inquiries that would be painful to
answer, but also as being in consonance
with feelings of loss and sorrow.

INDEX.

155